CARE OF THE HANDS AND NAILS

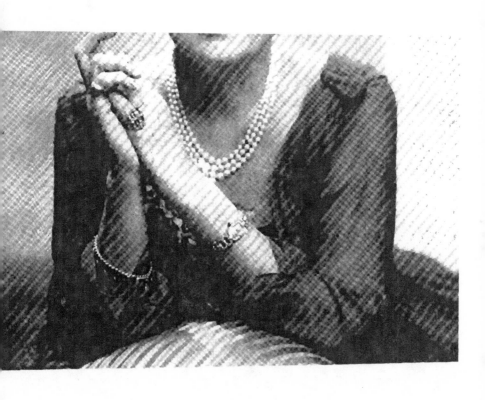

Coralie Godfrey

CARE OF THE
HANDS
AND
NAILS

CORALIE GODFREY

Contents

Illustrations

ACKNOWLEDGMENTS

To Mrs Garrard W. Glenn, for allowing her lovely hands and nails to be used as an inspiration; to my Staff, past and present, for their help and encouragement; and my gratitude to the late Dr Francis Brook whose interest in developing nail cultures proved of inestimable value in my research work; also appreciation to my husband, Lt Col W. Rawson-Hughes, O.B.E., M.C., who has devoted so much of his time to the Hand & Nail Culture Institute.

Introduction

In a lifetime of caring for hands and nails, I have become familiar with so many varied degrees of ugly, destroyed and tortured hands and nails that I marvel at the strength and tenacity of those ten well-tried friends which protect our finger-tips.

What would life be like without them, I wonder, enabling us, as they do, to pick up the tiniest objects and protect our sensitive finger-tips from all the hard and destructive things we touch every minute of the day.

Nature has indeed been kind in giving us almost a 'rose petal' in colour and design as a finger-tip covering, to help us in our myriad needs when using our fingers, and how we abuse her wonderful protectiveness, expecting those 'rose petals' to remain intact and lovely whilst we, in our ignorance, permit them to be battered into a remote resemblance of the perfect, beautiful nails we received at birth.

It is to enable the reader to restore the fine texture, shape and health of the hands and nails that I have written this manual in the hope that if you already have your finger-tips covered with 'rose petals' you will retain them, but if not, that my effort will, in some way, help towards this end.

Simply, the aim of this manual is to lay a foundation for constructive treatment, and all the terms used are in simple and easily understood language. The need for a manual on hand and nail culture has long existed. In setting down a *routine* for this culture I hope to be of service to those who wish to become experts; to those who seek further knowledge of their subject and to those suffering from nail disorders, I trust my efforts and life work will bring practical help.

CORALIE GODFREY

London 1961

I

NAILS

To possess a completely healthy and beautiful nail adds greatly to the attractiveness of either man or woman. Yet the average man or woman has no knowledge of how to correct nail faults or even how to keep their nails in perfect condition. It is well to make a study of this subject for no grooming is complete unless the hands and nails are included. In the past this has been difficult because no information has existed in detail on the care of the hands and nails, but now there seems to be no excuse, because a careful study of this method of hand and nail culture will enable everyone not only to take a pride in their hands and nails, but will give them so much detailed information that they will be able to maintain their hands and nails in perfect condition and correct the manicurist should she mutilate their nails during treatment.

This, surely, is a step forward, and it is well to remember that when a nail is healthy it follows that it is beautiful as well.

SIMPLE TERMS USED IN MANICURE

Nailplate: Oblong, curved, hard plate covering the finger-end.

Nailbed: Lies immediately below the nailplate.

Embryo nail: Soft, unformed nail lying underneath the cuticle.

Cuticle: A fold of skin surrounding the half moon and nailplate.

Free-edge: A greyish, white, or opaque margin at the finger-tip end of the nailplate.

Dividing line: A shadowy line which divides the pink part of the nailplate from the free-edge.

Hangnail: A small piece of detached skin usually near the cuticle.

Nail groove: Parallel grooves in which the nailplate fits.

Half moon: So called because of its shape; lies in immediate proximity to the cuticle.

Longitudinal ridge: A ridge extending from the cuticle to the free-edge.

Transverse ridge: A ridge extending from one nail groove to the other.

Plate 2a shows the nailplate enlarged. Points to note particularly are:

1 The nail grooves are nearly parallel and reach the finger-tip.

2 The nailplate is well embedded in the nail grooves and is rounded.

3 The free-edge of the nailplate commences near the finger-tip,

4 The half moon is fine and clear.

5 The shape of the cuticle, nailplate, half moon and free-edge is harmonious.

To restore troublesome nails and maintain normal ones here are three golden rules:

1 Never cut or file the corners of the nailplate away.

2 Never dig into the free-edge of the nailplate when cleaning.

3 Never push back the cuticle.

THE PERFECT NAIL. A perfect nail should grow with complete freedom through the cuticle down to the free-edge, just as a river flows smoothly along its bed. The cuticle should be an even fold of skin under which it is possible to pass the tip of an orange stick for just a small fraction of space. The nail grooves should be parallel and reach nearly to the tip of the finger. The nailplate should be well embedded

1 This beautiful hand, with perfect nails, is that of
Mrs Garrard W. Glenn, daughter of Sir John and Lady Mullens.

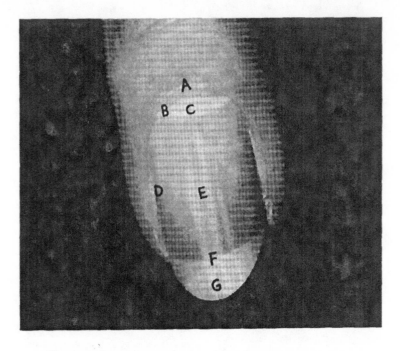

2a   The nailplate enlarged

A Embryo nail   B Cuticle   C Half moon   D Nail groove
E Pink part of nailplate   F Dividing line   G Free-edge

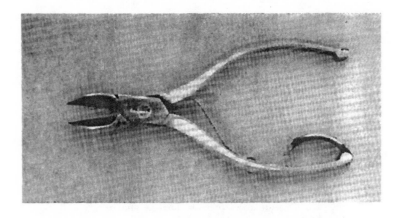

2b   Nail clippers

in the finger, with a perfect fold of flesh enveloping it. The pink part of the nail should reach nearly to the tip of the finger and should be a bright and clear colour. The nails themselves should be strong, slightly flexible, almond in shape with a not too large half moon; they should possess a shiny surface and the pink part of each nail should be in proportion to the pink part of the other nails.

HOW NAILS ARE FORMED. Nails can be compared, in their embryo state, to the hair. As the embryo nail grows out and is exposed to the air it hardens, becoming, in its finished state, a hard, shiny plate, with a smooth, outer surface. The nailplate rests on the nail bed, which gives it nourishment and perfect form. Nails usually take about six months to grow from their embryo state to the free-edge, and grow at a faster rate in summer than in winter.

THE UTILITY OF NAILS. Nails are formed as a complete protector to the tips of the fingers. They are impervious to weak alkalies and acids, but succumb to strong ones. Their function is to protect the sensitive finger-tips; they act as an aid in picking up small objects and can also be used most effectively as defensive weapons!

THE CIRCULATION OF THE NAILS. When a nail lies perfectly in its bed and conforms to its intended shape, fitting snugly into its groove, it plays an important part in the circulation, colour, and texture of the whole hand. The nail not only completes, but aids, the flow of blood in the finger-tips and, by taking its full complement of nutrition from the nail bed and hands, helps to clear away any congestion.

THE EFFECT OF BAD MANICURING. One bad manicure can cause much discomfort and trouble. A slight cut with an instrument which has not been properly disinfected can result in inflammation and poisoning which may take months to repair. A manicure should never be painful, and the practical and theoretical sides should both be completely mastered before any attempts are made to operate. It is better to leave the nails entirely alone than damage them through ignorance.

B

POISON AND NAILS. Ancient history tells us that one of the oldest forms of poisoning known was grated nail, which the villain of the piece surreptitiously slipped into the food or wine of the intended victim and one can observe how, even today we are very careful to disinfect a scratch caused by a nail. This caution is due to the almost superstitious belief that the nail contains poisoning properties. This belief, no doubt, exists owing to the nail containing a small percentage of arsenic. It is essential, therefore, that the manicurist should pay special attention to the cleaning and disinfecting of hands, nails, and instruments.

THE EMBRYO NAIL. The embryo nail lies under the cuticle in a soft, jelly state. Great care must be taken never to damage it as it is the most sensitive part of the nail. In some nails it lies nearer to the surface than in others and if a hard instrument is accidentally or deliberately dug into this part of the nail, the nail, being in a soft state, will be injured or dented, and will grow out with this malformation. If this damage is done regularly during a manicure a series of dents and cracks will show as the nails grow and will cause them to break when the malformation reaches the free-edge. If the dents and breaks are very deep the condition can be serious as it becomes a possible source of infection. The remedy naturally lies in never damaging the embryo nail and this is best attained by lifting up the cuticle without digging into the soft embryo nail immediately underneath it. Use an orange stick covered with cotton wool or a rubber ended hoof-stick for any manipulation necessary at that delicate part of the nail. Dents formed on the embryo nail take several months to grow out.

THE HALF MOON. This is an intermediate stage between the embryo nail and the hardened nailplate and is, for no accountable reason, sometimes prominent and sometimes not visible. When the embryo nail lies very near the cuticle the half moon is usually large and well defined and often soft and easily damaged. If the half moon is not well defined the embryo nail lies well back, and the nail immediately adjacent to the cuticle will be harder and less likely to be injured by exterior pressure. Pushing the cuticle back in order to make the half moon more prominent is the cause of many nail and cuticle troubles. It is noticeable that the half moon of the thumb nail is usually more prominent and softer than the other nails, but there seems to be no accountable reason for this difference in structure.

THE DIVIDING LINE. Great importance attaches to the dividing line. This is where the pink part of the nail finishes and the free-edge commences. This line usually appears to be a greyish colour, neither pink nor white, and it is owing to this peculiar shadowy grey that it is pushed back rigorously when the nail is cleaned: in the attempt to get rid of it, but no matter how much it is pushed or pressed back, or dug into, it *never* disappears; it only recedes further back, leaving more free-edge, less pink, and more room for grime to get in. It should not be touched when the nails are cleaned, for if this line is entirely left alone the nailplate will gradually adhere to the finger-tip and the nail will become a better shape.

It is interesting to note the formation of a new born baby's nails. These are what is termed 'square', and have no free-edge; the pink part reaches the extreme tip of the finger. It is only with use that the free-edge develops, as dirt gets in and is cleaned out.

Mechanical Treatment of the Nailplate

Should a nail be clipped or filed seems to be the first question asked when it is desired to shorten a nail. Quite definitely it should be clipped to length and initial shaping.

The nail lies snugly in its bed and if it is long and needs shortening – complete shortening by filing only, is liable to be injurious as, every time the file is moved backwards and forwards, it disturbs the nail bed. If you multiply this action many times and then compare it with three or four clips with the nail clippers you will realise that the clippers are less strain on the nailplate and quicker than filing (Plate 2b).

The spring on the clippers should be adjusted so that, when the clippers are held loosely in the palm of the right hand in an open position, the spring keeps the cutting edges half an inch apart. This is important as, when the clippers are used for clearing underneath the cuticle, this space is essential for effective scraping.

CLIPPING FOR LENGTH. Hold the nail clippers in your right hand with the curved edges facing the nail at right angles. The points of the nail clippers should be facing to the left. The handles of the clippers are controlled by the palm of the right hand and four fingers, the thumb resting near the spring. Practise closing and releasing the curved blades in order to get the 'feel' of controlling the blades.

At first, the handles of the clippers are liable to chafe the palm of the hand and make it sore. This is because the clippers are being held too tightly. With practice the clippers can be manipulated with perfect ease (Plate 3a).

Stop your practice for a moment and cut several long strips of paper half an inch wide (magazine paper is the best thickness). Start clipping small fragments of this as if it was a nail and keep on practising this until you feel you are efficient and can control the clippers with the palm of the hand and fingers. Then try clipping, for length only, your own nails and finally, someone else's nails: holding the nail to be clipped straight in front of you at a convenient level. You will find a difference when first changing from the paper to a real nail because the paper is flat, while the nail is rounded.

A normal, flexible nail can be shortened with one clip, but when the nails are thick and hard, two or more clips may be required – taking much smaller pieces of nail each time.

A word of warning here is necessary. Where you find a condition of the nailplate being completely attached to the finger-tip, right to the extreme edge, and where there is no free-edge (as in a new born baby's, and sometimes in adults) this type of nailplate is extremely sensitive – it bleeds easily, and should not be shortened by clipping. The soft side of an emery board should be used, to avoid injury and pain.

The most important part of manipulating nail clippers is to bring the top blade *down* to meet the underneath blade. This will allow the nailplate to remain in its normal position. If this operation is reversed and the underneath blade is brought upwards to meet the top blade (as so many beginners do) the nailplate will be forced upwards and the clipping will be uncomfortable and painful.

The nail should not be clipped shorter than the finger-tips as its function is to protect the finger-tip. If the nail is clipped too short the flesh of the finger-tip becomes sensitive, bulgy and uncontrolled. The nail should not be left too long as this causes strain, but it is preferable for a nail to be too long than too short.

In the case of very dry nails, and this frequently occurs in middle-aged and older people, the free-edge of the nailplate should be filled with a good emolient cream before clipping or filing. This will lesson the brittleness and the nailplate will not be so apt to split and end up with ragged edges. Well fill the free-edge of the nailplate with cream and proceed to clip and file as usual. There is more elasticity in the nails of young people and this precaution will not be found necessary.

When the clipping and filing is completed fill the free-edge of the nailplate again with emolient cream, and it is essential for very dry nails that the free-edge of the nailplate is always full of nourishment to avoid further deterioration and splitting, especially after washing the hands. Plate 3b shows how a nail should look after the first clip.

CLIPPING FOR SHAPE. Hold your clippers, as before, in the palm of your right hand lightly, with the cutting edges in an open position. Place them in a slanting position on the right-hand side of the free-edge of the nail and clip a piece of the free-edge away to act as a base for your oval shaping later on with a file. Now reverse the clippers and clip away a piece of the free-edge from the left-hand side of the nailplate. Practise this on paper first for some considerable time before attempting to clip a real nail.

The clipping must be on the free-edge of the nail only, and

care must be exercised to keep the clippers in such a position that they do not clip into the pink part of the nail. The clipped nail should show an even form, with the same amount clipped from each side. Plate 4a shows how a nail should look after the second and third clip.

FILING THE NAILS. Filing should be done with an unplated long file measuring 6 to 8 inches and triple cut. See Plate 4b.

Hold the file lightly between the thumb and fingers. It should be manipulated very gently, with short movements, from right to left and not used backwards and forwards vigorously, as so many manicurists do, because vigorous filing disturbs the nail bed. The file should not be rested on the flesh of the finger-tip but be controlled so that it touches the nailplate only. Plate 5a shows how to hold the file.

The nail, after clipping for shape, has four points and if the four points are gently filed away the correct shape will result. After filing with the steel file an under-edge will be left on the extreme tip of the free-edge. Use an emery board to remove this. The emery board will also give a smoother edge than a steel file and should always be used to finish the shaping. Some nails are so sensitive that a steel file is unbearable. In such cases use an emery board for the whole operation.

FILING FOR SHAPE. The shape of the nail should be in harmony with the general contour of the whole nail and cuticle and can be round, oval or almond in shape.

When the pink part of the nailplate is uneven, or lower on one side than the other, the missing pink should be allowed for and the nail shaped as if it were there. This will allow the separated portion, providing it is not dug into, to continue its work of adhering to the finger.

The shape of the nail depends very much on the treatment it receives. If the corners of the nailplate are cut, or filed away, the nail will become detached from its bed and grooves and will be splay and flat. By allowing the corners to grow up the nail will become attached to the finger and, as the finger is round, the nail will become curved and almond shaped and will lose its flat, splay shape, also the nail grooves will become parallel as the splay shape gradually disappears. Plate 5b shows a nail after clipping and filing.

To shape one's own nails and to leave the corners well embedded, press the finger flat out on a table, nailplate upwards, and with an emery board, or file, shape the nail by placing the file on the outside of the flesh which surrounds the nailplate. As the file is brought forward in the filing movement the flesh prevents the nailplate being filed away at the corners and the nail will retain its natural shape.

Polishing the Nailplate

A nail, to look its best, must either be polished with a buffer or finished with a coat of nail enamel.

BUFFING. When buffing the nail, move the buffer *one way only*; do not move it backwards and forwards because the movement both ways causes friction and the nailplate will become hot. This friction heat is very bad for the nailplate and will make the nails dry and brittle.

The best polishing medium is a stone or powder. This is rubbed on the chamois leather of the buffer and not on the nailplate, and is then applied by rubbing the nailplate with the buffer. The chamois should be frequently washed and a better result is always obtained with a fresh leather, a liberal amount of the polishing medium and a nailplate free from grease.

APPLYING NAIL ENAMEL. Nail enamel completely seals the nail and dries it up. It is immaterial whether the enamel is of good, or bad, quality. All enamels are definitely bad for nails over a period of time, but if used with care little harm will result. Some nails will withstand the effects of enamel for years, while for some it will be a matter of weeks or months before the nails become 'flaky', brittle, and break.

If the nails are very strong, enamel should be renewed at least twice a week, as the elasticity of the enamel and that of the nail is not the same. This means that when the nail bends with daily wear and tear, tiny, almost invisible, cracks appear in the enamel which wear a corresponding fine line in the nailplate and eventually cause it to break but, with renewing the enamel frequently, this trouble is minimised as the new enamel does not develop the tiny cracks for a day or two.

If enamel is used frequently and no bad results have appeared it is still advisable to give the nails a complete rest for two or three weeks at a time, at least twice a year. Leave all enamel off and apply a good nail food at night, and wear gloves. When the nails are flaky, brittle, and break off – enamel must be dispensed with altogether until they have completely recovered. This will take from two to six months and sometimes longer.

Give the nails plenty of nourishment and keep them short. File the flaky pieces with an emery board and when the nails have recovered and it is desired to use nail enamel again – remove the enamel each night in order to give the nailplate some nourishment.

There are many fads and fancies with regard to applying nail enamel. Enamels vary and it is only by experience that one finds out the best method of application. The nail must be absolutely clear and free from grease, otherwise the enamel will not adhere to the nailplate. The enamel must not only be allowed to dry but to harden right through, and it is advisable to refrain from putting on gloves, or using the hands and nails for at least 15 to 20 minutes after applying the enamel so that it may harden and set. Usually the best results when using deep colours are obtained by applying two coats.

It is better if the half moon is left clear. The free-edge may be entirely covered, or not, according to individual taste.

Nail enamel, once the bottle is opened, will dry up and go thick – some quicker than others. This is due to evaporation. The cap should, therefore, be screwed on immediately after use. If the enamel becomes very thick and unusable a few drops of enamel remover will thin it down and make it usable again. If the screw top becomes stuck, place it under a hot water tap; the heat will make the enamel pliable and it can be opened easily by hand or with a nutcracker, anti-clockwise. On some nails enamel wears better if a tiny portion of enamel is removed from the extreme tip of the free-edge. This is called removing a hair-line margin and should be done with a soft paper tissue while the enamel is wet.

In cases where, over a period of time, the nail has dried up, or is brittle and breaking, a pleasing effect can be obtained, with less injury to the nailplate, by painting a line of enamel down the centre of the nailplate – not wider than the width of the enamel brush – on the pink part only. This leaves the half moon, free-edge and each side of the nail-plate clear to absorb nail foods. This method is only possible with natural, or pale pink enamels, which tone in with the surrounding colour of the nailplate. Deep colours of enamel do not lend themselves to this method of application.

The teenager would do well to use pale coloured enamels. Youth is so attractive in itself that it needs little embellishment and a pale pink nail enamel, either a coral or shell pink tone, is best suited to the teenager. It is the 20 to 40 age group who can really go all out for brilliant colours. The chic and sophisticated women of that age group can use all the bright and lovely shades ranging from the orange reds to shocking pink and the deep rich tones of pillar box red and crimson. All these attractive colours should harmonise with the lipstick worn. Nothing is so unattractive as a brilliant coloured nail enamel and a lipstick which does not harmonise.

Many of the well-known manufacturers of beauty products specialise in blending colours to match lipsticks with their nail enamels and there are many manufacturers who make a beautiful range of colours with this purpose in view. Nowadays so many women remain attractive, soignée and well groomed right into old age and many continue using exotic colours but, when the hair turns grey and then white, and the hands become 'old' and wrinkled, a woman should use the delicate colours she wore as a teenager. Deep red nail enamel of all tones makes the hands look older and claw-like and adds nothing to an elderly woman's charm.

Very young schoolgirls should be discouraged from using nail enamel except on party occasions as their nails are not so tough as in later life. Nail enamel is not suitable for a delicate nailplate such as is found on very young children. For party occasions a clear, colourless enamel is best suited to the very young and it should be removed immediately the party is over.

When buying nail enamel it is advisable to buy a range of five or six colours and one bottle of natural enamel to mix paler shades when desired. Nail enamel should tone, not only with your lipstick but with your whole ensemble. For instance, an orange red nail enamel, shocking pink lipstick and pillar box red dress would not show good taste, so blend your nail enamel to tone with your colour scheme and keep as many shades as you can in your beauty box for this purpose.

You may find on an occasion that none of the shades of nail enamel that you have are suitable for the dress you intend to wear, but you will be able to mix a shade yourself from the various colours you possess. One thing is important: always mix nail enamel that is manufactured by the same firm. If you decide to buy a certain make of nail enamel buy all your various colours from the same manufacturer because, although all nail enamel looks the same, no matter what the make, every manufacturer uses a different formula. If you mix two different formulas you will have a completely unstaple article and your effort will have been wasted.

Use an old empty nail enamel bottle and add two or three colours to choice. Well mix and stir with an orange stick. It is better not to shake the enamel as that would create air bubbles which will transfer themselves to the nailplate when you apply the enamel and prevent an even, smooth surface.

It is worth a little trouble to obtain the attractive, harmonious effect of nails, colour scheme and make-up being as perfect as you can make them.

ENAMEL REMOVERS. A good remover for nail enamel should be non-acetone and contain oil. Even then all enamel removers are bad for the nailplate and cuticle as they have a drying effect and, over a period of time, destroy the natural elasticity of the nail. This can be lessened to some extent by immediately applying a good nail emolient after using the enamel remover. This will counteract the drying properties of the remover.

A small piece of cotton wool should be saturated with the remover and held for a second on the nailplate to soften the enamel, then rub the nailplate firmly with downward strokes to remove the softened enamel, carefully avoiding the cuticle. Immediately afterwards apply an emolient and leave it on the nailplate while you proceed with the next nail, starting always with the little finger and working towards the thumb. Do both hands in this way, then take a fresh piece of cotton wool and wipe each nail clear of emolient. You should now have the nails clear and free of enamel. When the enamel is a very deep colour this procedure will need to be repeated two or three times.

Keep the enamel remover well corked as it evaporates very rapidly, be careful not to spill the remover on furniture or fabrics as it will remove the surface and colour. Enamel remover will sting if allowed to come in contact with an open cut or hangnail, and the manicurist should avoid as much as possible having her own nails in contact with it when operating.

STAIN REMOVER. An efficient stain remover should remove ink and iodine stains and also clean the free-edge of the nailplate. Stain removers are slightly drying to the skin and should be used sparingly. A good one should be non-injurious: it should be used in exactly the same way as enamel remover.

For the free-edge of the nailplate, wrap the tip of an orange stick in cotton wool and dip it into the remover, then gently clean under the free-edge of the nailplate, taking care not to dig into the dividing line which separates the free-edge from the body of the nail.

Lemon juice is an excellent, quick, and simple cleaner. To make a cleaner and stain remover which will keep indefinitely and which will remove ink and iodine stains, add ½ oz. ammonia and 4 ozs. of pure lemon juice to 4 ozs. of weak peroxide. Bottle into airtight bottles and leave about 1 inch of space at the top of the bottle to allow room for expansion of the remover. Do not shake the bottle.

Nail Irregularities

ACCIDENTAL INJURIES. When a nail is injured, such as being jammed in a door or window, it will usually recover and become normal again in a few months providing the damage is to the nailplate only, but if the injury goes deep enough to injure the nail bed then the malformation of the nail will be permanent as the nail receives its perfect form from the bed in which it lies. In both cases protection and exterior nourishment of the finger-tip are necessary.

SHOCK. It is interesting to see the effect shock can have on the nails and it is generally possible to determine the approximate month the shock occurred as the embryo nail will register marks at the time of the shock, often in the form of a transverse dent or ridge. As the nail grows the marks caused by the shock will be clearly seen and will move with the growth of the nail towards the free-edge. As it takes six months for the full growth of the nail from the cuticle to the free-edge the approximate month of the shock can be determined from the position of the marks. A shock such as the death of a relative, a high temperature, and other reactions in the blood stream during an illness are frequent causes of unusual marks, but they are only temporary and eventually disappear.

SEPARATION OF THE NAILPLATE. Nails which have become separated from their bed more than they normally should be can usually be greatly improved with corrective treatment. The condition can be caused by using a nail brush too vigorously which encourages the nailplate to separate from the finger. Digging the fingers into clay, earth or any substance, long immersion in soap and water, and too much pressure when cleaning the nails are other causes.

When the condition is self-inflicted the nails should be left entirely alone for several months and not cleaned at all except with a sponge and soapy lather. The pink part of the nail will gradually re-attach itself and grow towards the free-edge and there will not be the space for dirt to collect.

Treatment for separation of the nailplate due to nail disorders will be found in Chapter 6.

OCCUPATIONAL DISORDERS. Unfortunately there are many occupations which directly cause nail troubles and it is obvious that household, cooking, gardening, nursing etc. are contributory factors as well as such substances as water, soap, flour, lime, pastes, sugar, grease, yeasts, acids, alkalies, starch, disinfectants, paints and dyes.

If the nails are weak and susceptible to any of these products, and a nail disorder has developed, it would be wise to change one's occupation if this is at all possible. When this is not practicable every precaution and care should be taken to counter these working conditions.

CLEARING STAINS FROM THE NAILPLATE. Coloured nail enamels, household cleaning agents and acidity are some causes of discoloured nails. When purchasing nail enamel choose one which does not stain the nails. Enamels which are coloured with *pigmented* colouring matter are usually non-staining. Some nail enamels are coloured with dyes which dissolve and the dye sinks into the nailplate. Nails sometimes appear with yellow, brown, black and various coloured stains on them.

If a small portion of the nail is scraped with the blade edge of a pair of scissors by gentle downward strokes from half moon to free-edge and if the nail underneath appears free from stain and is pink and healthy, then all the nails should have the stain removed by this mechanical means. Take long, sweeping, light movements downwards from the half moon to the free-edge and, where the nail is rounded and the angle becomes difficult, file the stain away with an emery board, and finish cleaning the nailplate all over with the emery board. The nails will then look dull but free from stains and they may then be polished with a buffer and suitable polishing agent and will immediately regain their shiny surface.

When the stains are right through all the layers of nail the above method is useless and the nail must be allowed to grow out. While this is in progress an enamel may be used to cover up the blemishes, but it must be a non-staining one or the trouble will continue.

Some stains are caused by rheumatism or acidity which give the nails a yellowish or greyish tinge. Here is a restorative treatment. First, remove a thin outer layer of nail as directed above: soak the nails for 15 to 20 minutes in hot water to open the pores, then apply iodine X all over the nailplate and let it soak in and dry. Use this treatment last thing at night and do not wash the hands again for 8 to 12 hours. Next day, at the first washing of the hands, most of the discoloration from iodine X will disappear and the nails will gradually lose their yellowish tinge and become more pink and normal-looking. This is a wonderful health-giving treatment but should not be used more than five or six times a year.

A good nail food should be applied every night afterwards as iodine X has a tendency to dry the nailplate. It is advisable to keep the nails short during this treatment. Where there is an allergy to iodine, pure lemon juice can be used but this will not have the health-giving, toning and clearing effect of the iodine.

CLIMATE. A cold, crisp climate can cause nails to break and flake. In reverse, a warm or hot climate will help the nails to grow long and strong. These conditions are brought about by the circulation and the influence of hot, or cold extremes on the blood stream. Massage, wax baths and warm, loose gloves are a great help in cold weather, while attention should be given to the circulation of the whole body.

DIET. Diet, in some cases, proves of considerable help in weak and brittle nails. Naturally, a diet deficient in protein, calcium or vitamins, and lacking balance, will impair the general health; nails and hair cannot obtain the nourishment necessary to their formation and sustenance. Lack of calcium is the most important factor where nails are concerned. A natural source of calcium is dried skim milk. Calcium in tablet form can be taken in suitable doses under the directions of a doctor and does, in some cases, completely clear up nail troubles, but it is not always successful.

In any event, a sensible and well-balanced diet, with plenty of protein, salads and fruit, is necessary if the body is to be maintained in a healthy condition and the nails to receive their full complement of nourishment. Vitamins B and D are the two most important factors for nail nourishment.

WATER. Hard, chalky drinking water is a frequent cause of breaking nails. This should be counteracted by using a good, bottled Spa water for some months until the nails recover. Hard water for washing too is often the cause of brittle nails. This can be overcome by using a suitable water softener.

If the nails are in a bad condition they should be kept entirely out of water. Rubber gloves should be worn in the bath and for all purposes where water is used.

The disastrous effects of water on nails cannot be stressed too strongly. When immersion in water is unavoidable a good emollient should be used afterwards.

Nail Care for Children and Babies

It is a good idea to interest children in the care of their

hands and nails, as many nail troubles can be avoided later if this is done. When the child is a few months old it is naturally the mother's duty to see that her baby's nails are not allowed to be too long, as small babies are apt to cut or irritate their skin unconsciously if they have nails that are too long. A baby's hands should be well dried after washing and a little emolient cream or lotion applied, and the nails should be kept short and square. This is best accomplished by using the soft side of an emery board.

The cuticles should be left entirely alone because the embryo nail is in a very jelly-like, soft condition and can easily be damaged. The nailplate itself is thin, sensitive and delicate. The adult caring for the baby's nails should, therefore, be most gentle when attending to them.

As the child grows older the embryo nail and nailplate will harden and then a rubber-ended hoof stick can be used gently on the cuticles. Any dirt in the free-edge of the nail should be removed with cotton wool and an orange stick and an emolient applied to the cuticles to prevent hangnails.

When the child is about seven years of age it should be given some simple manicure implements such as emery boards, orange sticks, a rubber-ended hoof stick and nail emolient. Never give a child steel or any kind of metal manicure set: it will do more harm than good. Show the child how to look after its own nails with the above mentioned articles and, if a little girl, encourage her with a tiny buffer to polish the nails – one way only. This early training will ensure an awareness of the necessity of caring about their hands and nails.

From the age of seven an occasional professional manicure will be helpful, providing the treatment is gentle, once every three months would be ample. Children at school should be taken once or twice during their holidays for professional treatment to an experienced manicurist, and encouraged during term time to keep their hands and nails well groomed.

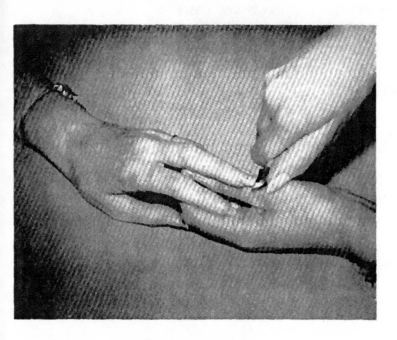

3a How to hold the nail clippers

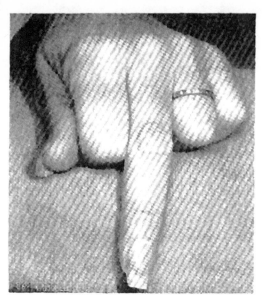

3b
A nail clipped
for length

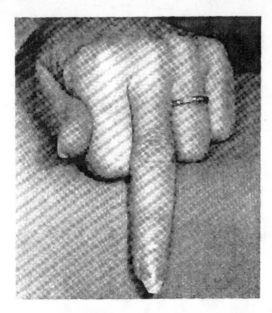

4a
A nail clipped
for shape

4b   A nail file

2
CUTICLES

c

The most outstanding and interesting part of the following method for the treatment of cuticles is the discovery, from experience, that it is possible permanently to restore growing cuticles so that they never grow again. This is something unique in the treatment of cuticles and no other method has ever solved this difficult problem.

The theoretical and mechanical part of the treatment is of great importance and is described step by step in order that it can be clearly understood. A healthy and beautiful nail depends on a perfect cuticle. If the cuticle is growing, dry, ragged, red or swollen the whole contour of the nail will be distorted. We are so misguided in our early youth about cuticles and taught to care for them in such an erroneous way that it is no wonder so many of us suffer from uncomfortable cuticles. We are born with perfect cuticles and it is entirely our own fault if we lose them through incorrect probing and treatment.

If you have good, healthy cuticles and a naturally well-nourished skin all the cuticles will need is a daily emolient. If not, a study of this chapter will correct cuticle faults and show you how to maintain the cuticle in a healthy and attractive condition.

THE PERFECT CUTICLE. This is a natural fold of skin completely surrounding the nailplate. It should have a small, fine rim surrounding the half moon. This fine rim should be clear, even, and unattached to the nailplate.

Some fortunate possessors of a well-nourished skin have

a perfect cuticle naturally, but others, owing to occupation, health, neglect or ignorance are continually troubled with bad cuticles: a most unsightly condition and one which not only ruins the whole appearance of the hand but can become a source of infection.

FUNCTION OF THE CUTICLE. The natural function of the cuticle is to protect the live flesh in which the nail is embedded. When the cuticle is broken, ragged or neglected, the live flesh is exposed to exterior damage. Constant care is necessary in order to maintain the natural function of the cuticle.

PUSHING BACK THE CUTICLE. The first thing we are told about our cuticles when we are young is to push them back with the towel every time we wash and dry our hands. Nothing could be more injurious to the cuticle or nail. Hangnails, inflammation and whitlows result from this habit.

The cuticle should never be pushed back with a towel or any instrument. When drying the hands care should be taken to use a downward movement from the knuckles to the finger-tips so that the cuticle is not disturbed in any way.

HOW THE CUTICLE AFFECTS THE SHAPE OF THE NAIL. It is not generally realised that if a cuticle becomes stuck to the nail, irregular, inflamed and troublesome, the shape of the nail suffers in consequence. When the cuticle is clear and free, the nail is unfettered and can retain its rounded shape, but with the cuticle stuck to it, it is unable to do this and consequently it loses its natural roundness and becomes smaller, flatter looking and uneven in shape. The cuticle should be kept completely free and clear from the nail. Daily care is the best way.

LIQUID ACID CUTICLE REMOVERS. Liquid cuticle removers, by artificially removing the cuticle, expose the delicate live tissues and can be most harmful. The cuticle should not be removed in this way, but removed mechanically, and afterwards kept in a healthy condition by the application of a bland emolient such as Healthinale.

Some Types of Cuticles

NORMAL CUTICLES. Normal cuticles give very little trouble. The perfect and well-nourished fold surrounding the nailplate requires no mechanical treatment; all it needs is a good cuticle emolient once or twice a day after washing the hands. Otherwise it should be left entirely alone.

DRY CUTICLES. These are often caused by acidity and rheumatism and this shows in the form of a dry, white deposit underneath or near the cuticle. The fold of the cuticle should be gently lifted and the deposit removed mechanically by a professional. The cuticle can then be kept in a more comfortable condition by using a rubber-ended hoof stick every day with a cuticle emolient, and so prevent the deposit from forming again and the cuticle from being dry and uncomfortable.

The lack of natural oil in these cases is replaced by the emolient which should be asceptic and health giving. At the same time the emolient should nourish the embryo nail and nailplate.

CUTICLES WHICH STICK TO THE NAIL. This condition is most troublesome and uncomfortable. In addition to dryness and an acid deposit the cuticles stick to the nail. The nail grows and pulls the cuticle with it, but the cuticle cannot stretch beyond a certain point, with the result that when it reaches this point, it breaks and this causes hangnails, inflammation and ragged, torn cuticles. Where this condition exists the cuticles should be gently released by lifting them up with a trimmer.

The deposit under the cuticle should be mechanically removed by an expert and the cuticles kept free and clear of the nailplate by daily applications of an emolient inserted underneath the cuticle. This will prevent the cuticle adhering to the nailplate and it will not grow stuck down to the nail again. Full details of the method for the mechanical treatment of the cuticles will be found later in this chapter.

THICK GROWING CUTICLES. This condition is most unsightly and requires much patience and perseverance to overcome. When the cuticle is stuck to the nail, release this by inserting the trimmer, then clear the debris from underneath the cuticle by scraping the debris away with the cuticle and nail clippers.

If it is not possible to complete the lifting and clearing of this type of cuticle in one operation then repeat all the movements gently as many times as necessary until the cuticle is completely free of the nailplate. Now you are faced with a thick, unattached cuticle which, unfortunately, must be cut. But, before doing this, the cuticles must be stretched mechanically to make them finer. This must be done expertly (see STRETCHING THE CUTICLE). After carefully stretching the cuticle, it must be correctly cut so that all further growth is discouraged and a gradual diminishing takes place. With correct treatment and daily care it is possible to restore the cuticles permanently so that they will never grow again.

PERMANENT DIMINISHING OF THE CUTICLE. Nature gave the cuticle a narrow, dead, perfect rim to act as a protection for the live flesh. When this is completely cut away the cuticle immediately grows again and each time it is cut the cuticle grows thicker and more unsightly. To permanently diminish this type of cuticle the preparation should be the same as for other types of cuticles. The cuticle should be released with the trimmer and the deposit cleared away mechanically. The cuticle may then need stretching if it is thick.

The next step is important. The amount of cuticle cut or trimmed away must be only *one half* of the width of the dead, lifted cuticle. The trimming or cutting should leave the other half of the dead rim as nature intended, to protect the live flesh. After cutting or trimming, the dead rim which is left should have an even, smooth edge.

The dead lifted cuticle should be trimmed or cut away with cuticle clippers. Scissors should not be used as they have a tendency to cut too much and too far. The even, dead rim surrounding the cuticle must now be kept free and clear of

the nailplate and an emolient applied twice a day underneath it – using an orange stick, the tip of which is wrapped
in cotton wool.

Every seven days the mechanical part of the treatment
can be repeated. Providing the cuticle is kept free and clear
in the interval, the dead rim surrounding the cuticle will
become less and less; and finer with each treatment, and
eventually will not grow again.

If the dead, lifted rim of the cuticle is cut or trimmed
away completely and no dead rim is left surrounding the
live flesh and protecting it then the cuticle will grow faster
and thicker than before. With each successive treatment
permanent improvement is clearly visible.

The mechanical treatment of the cuticle should be fully
studied and practised for some considerable time before any
attempt is made to lift, clear, stretch, cut or trim the cuticle,
as careless or inexpert treatment can do immeasurable harm
both to cuticles and embryo nail.

STRETCHING THE CUTICLE. When the cuticles are very
thick and troublesome and are trimmed or cut in that condition naturally the result is less cuticle but the thickness
remains. In order to gradually obtain a fine, thin cuticle,
careful stretching of the cuticles is necessary before cutting
them. This is done by using the cuticle clippers in such a
way that they stretch the cuticle instead of cutting it.

To do this, place the cuticle clippers on the thick rim,
bring the blade edges of the clippers together so that they
hold the cuticle but do not cut it – then pull the thick cuticle
gently towards you so that you stretch it, and in this way
keep on stretching the cuticle in small pieces without cutting.
When the cuticle is stretched to about double its original
width it will be thinner and may then be cut, as outlined in
the Method for Permanent diminishing of the cuticle. The
result will be a finer cuticle rim. Do this each time the cuticle
is treated, about once in seven days. Gradually the cuticle
rim will diminish and eventually stop its forward growth;
getting finer with each successive treatment.

The mechanical operation of stretching the cuticles is only suitable on thick, hard, growing cuticles and should not be used on normal, or thin cuticles as this treatment used when unnecessary will split the delicate cuticle. A cuticle emollient should be used several times a day, and at night, after this treatment.

CUTTING THE CUTICLE. Cutting the cuticle should be avoided as much as possible and resorted to only when a cuticle has been cut before and is in a bad condition owing to previous cutting; and then only for the minimum time, to allow the cuticle to return to normal. Cutting a cuticle which has never been cut before is deplorable, for the cuticle will immediately start to grow.

A cuticle clipper may be used to trim small pieces of cuticle which are out of alignment or where the cuticle is split, frayed or ragged. In cases where the cuticle has been cut and is growing, it is not possible to effect a cure without temporarily cutting them. This cutting, however, should cease immediately the cuticle has permanently diminished and the natural rim is in evidence.

After opening, scraping and, where necessary, stretching, the cuticle should only be cut when absolutely essential, always leaving a thin, even rim to protect the live flesh. Normal and delicate cuticles should never be cut and should be treated with the utmost care.

SPLITS AND CRACKS OF THE CUTICLE. Splits and cracks are caused by allowing the cuticle to stick to the nailplate. They should be cut or clipped short and collodion applied, or a little iodine X. They can be kept in check if the cuticle is kept in a healthy condition and not allowed to adhere to the nail.

PERSISTENT ADHERENCE OF THE CUTICLE. In very difficult and persistent cases of the cuticle sticking to the nail, the following treatment has been found of inestimable value. First, soak the cuticles in a bowl of hot water, then lift, scrape, and give the cuticles a complete treatment. When this is finished lift each cuticle with a trimmer and trickle

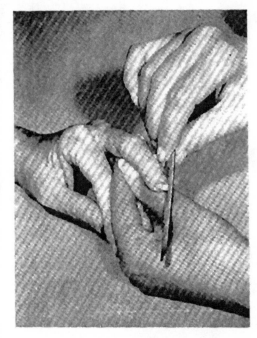

5a
How to hold the
nail file

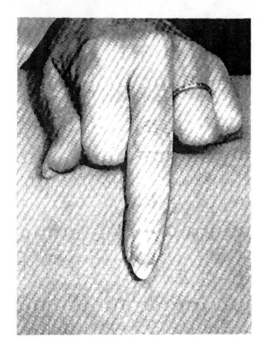

5b
A nail after clipping
and filing

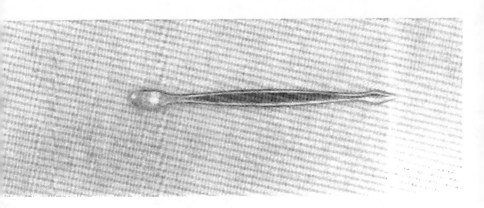

6a A trimmer

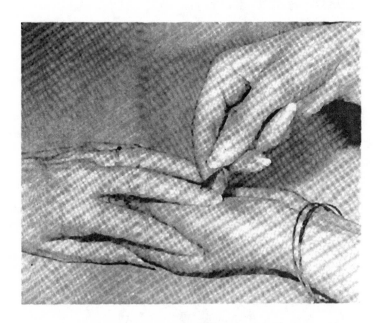

6b How to hold the trimmer

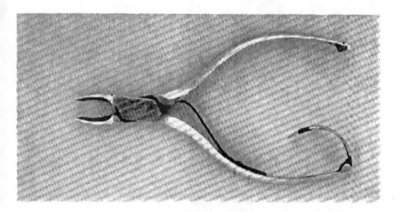

7a Cuticle clippers

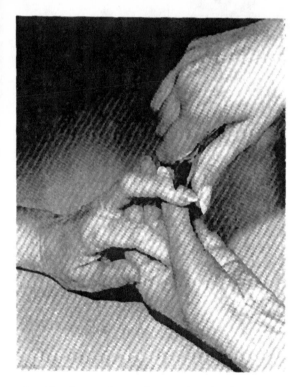

7b Clearing underneath the left half of the cuticle
with nail clippers

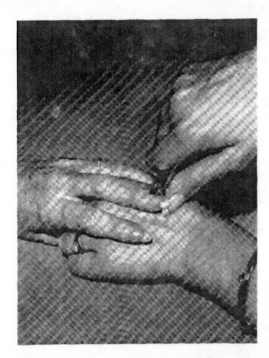

8a
Clearing underneath
the right half of the
cuticle with
cuticle clippers

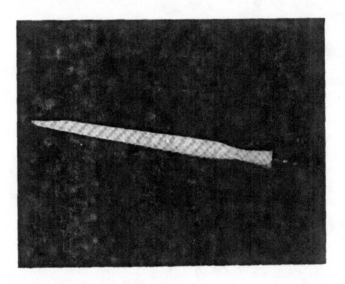

8b A hoof stick

collodion or clear enamel underneath it. Keep the nail in a horizontal position to allow a better flow of collodion to penetrate underneath the cuticle.

When the collodion is dry it will act as a barrier between the cuticle and the nailplate, and prevent the cuticle sticking to the nail. The treatment should be gentle and may be employed every seventh day until the cuticle is normal. In addition, cuticle emolient should be used two or three times a day.

DRY METHOD FOR CUTICLES. As a general rule the cuticles should be treated with the dry method. The cuticles should never be soaked unless they are very stuck to the nailplate. Cuticle disinfectant can be liberally applied to replace the soaking.

The dry method of treating the cuticle is undoubtedly the best as, when the nails are soaked, they become spongy, and the manicurist is liable to take away more than is necessary. A surgeon never soaks the part on which he intends to operate as, obviously, this would make the part more sensitive and spongy, and would not help the operation. The old method of manicure, which comprised soaking in water and soapsuds, is not only bad for the cuticles and nails but also for the manicurist's work, as she is unable to see what she is doing owing to the cuticle being covered in soap suds.

WET METHOD FOR CUTICLES. Occasionally it is necessary to employ the wet method when the cuticles are very stuck. They should be soaked in hot, soapy water for a few minutes and wiped dry before being lifted with the trimmer. When they are cured, use the dry method.

Mechanical Treatment of the Cuticles

LIFTING THE CUTICLE WITH A TRIMMER. This operation is necessary in order to open up the cuticle in readiness for scraping away the acid usually found there. It is performed with a small instrument called a trimmer (see Plate 6a). The blunt end of the trimmer is the operative end. The cuticle should be very gently lifted with the trimmer by holding the blunt end at the right-hand side of the nail and working it gently underneath the cuticle in small lifting movements from right to left.

The blunt end of the trimmer should be facing towards the left side of the nail and not in a direct angle towards the centre of the cuticle (see Plate 6b). Exceptional care must be exercised so that the embryo nail is not pressed into with the trimmer. If this is not done considerable damage will result to the soft embryo nail which lies underneath the cuticle edge.

The movement of the trimmer is to gently lift the cuticle up and away from the nail without pressing into the nail-plate. If the trimmer faces as shown in the illustration and is used correctly and gently the nailplate will not be injured.

SCRAPING UNDERNEATH THE CUTICLE. Scraping near the edge of the cuticle and slightly underneath it is most beneficial and if done expertly will release the cuticle and free the nails from acid and deposits, and has a lasting effect on the general comfort of the finger-tips.

Two pairs of clippers are necessary – a pair of nail clippers and a pair of cuticle clippers. Both cuticle and nail clippers have blades with curved edges; cuticle clippers (Plate 7a) have blades with an outward curved edge and nail clippers have blades with an inward curved edge.

One edge of the clipper blade is used in short, downward, semi-circular strokes to scrape and clear the acid deposit near and underneath the cuticle, the clippers being tilted and held so that the other blade does not touch the nailplate at all.

After the trimmer has prepared the cuticle by lifting it, hold the nail clippers with blades apart as shown in Plate 7b and commence at the centre of the cuticle, using the inward curved blade of the nail clippers to clear the left half of the cuticle. Then change to the cuticle clippers and use these to clear the right half of the cuticle (Plate 8a).

The deposit seen so clearly in some nails is scraped away without pressing into the nailplate. The movements must be light, precise, and controlled. Long practice on very strong nails, or practise on yourself, is the best way to learn. The curved blade of the nail clippers will be found to fit exactly the natural curve of the cuticle on the left side; the same applies to the right side of the cuticle, using the blade of the cuticle clippers. During this operation the cuticle and nail should be constantly damped with a mild liquid disinfectant. This will not only facilitate the scraping but is a necessary hygienic precaution. Apply the disinfectant to the cuticle with the tip of an orange stick wrapped in cotton wool.

This operation may be done with benefit every seven days and should be restricted to the debris round and underneath the cuticle. The entire nailplate should not be scraped.

Some nails have little, or no, deposit. After lifting and moistening with weak disinfectant they should be pressed gently into place with a hoof stick, to shape them, and scraping omitted altogether.

A hoof stick (Plate 8b) has a rubber hoof at one end and its gentle action is preferable for sensitive, delicate cuticles.

3
HANDS

We cannot all have perfect hands, but we can have well cared for and well groomed hands and, no matter how rough our daily work may be, we can protect them and remedy the injury done to them by our daily tasks. To dash out into the open on a cold winter's day without gloves is asking for trouble, while to expect the hands to stand up to all kinds of hard work without care is to expect a miracle.

The instructions following should be carefully carried out if you wish to improve and keep your hands in a state of health and beauty.

General Treatment

Much can be done to improve the hands but the treatment should be regular. Always wear gloves to do any work which tends to soil the hands – nice large ones, so that the circulation is not impeded.

Sometimes gloves worn at night are irritating. When this happens try treating one hand only at a time on alternate nights. This leaves one hand free, which is more bearable and comfortable. Gloves used at night should be frequently washed, as most creams contain a percentage of moisture. Damp gloves are not good for the hands and can cause the knuckles to swell.

Rubber gloves should be worn for all work where it is necessary to protect the hands from soap, soda, hot water, disinfectants, detergents etc., but care must be taken not to wear them a moment longer than is necessary, as rubber causes the hands to perspire and draws the natural oils out of the skin. This can, to some extent, be avoided by wearing a thin pair of cotton gloves inside the rubber ones, or using rubber gloves which have a sprayed inner cotton lining.

Clean the hands after any rough work with a good cream soap substitute. This is not so hard on the skin as soap and water; and apply a good emollient cream afterwards. When the hands are really grimed – massage olive oil into them first to loosen the dirt, and wipe it off with paper tissues. After this wash the hands in the normal way. If the hands are very stiff, massage them well every day with a good cream and exercise the hands and fingers by opening and closing and stretching the fingers as far as you can and, above all, keep them out of water.

Hands age more quickly than any other part of the body and should be given plenty of care and attention to keep them healthy and attractive. Use the best quality super-fatted soap, soap substitute, emollient cream or lotion. Avoid glycerine or glycerine products which have the effect of improving the skin temporarily but will, in time, coarsen the skin and make the hands red.

WASHING THE HANDS. Washing the hands is important. The water should be warm, not hot; very hot water takes the natural oils out of the skin. The water should be softened with a good water softener and not ordinary bath salts which, often, are only coloured soda.

Make a soapy lather on a cup-shaped sponge and proceed as if you were washing a baby's hand. Get a good lather into the free-edge of the nailplate as well as all over the hand and proceed with a suction movement at the nail tips for a few seconds. Do not use a nail brush, as this detaches the nail-plate from the finger. Rinse the hands, well dry them and apply a few drops of lotion or cream.

CARE OF NORMAL HANDS. If the skin of your hands is soft and the fingers are flexible a light cream or lotion, after washing, will be found sufficient to keep them in good order.

Occasionally massage a good nourishing cream into the hands at night and wear loose gloves.

DRY HANDS. When the hands are dry and uncomfortable considerable care is necessary to keep them from deteriorating. A good heavy feeding cream should be applied every night and gloves worn. The hands should be washed as little as possible and, for quick relief, wash them with soap and water only twice a day: morning and evening, and use an emolient afterwards.

During the day clean them with a cream soap substitute. Rub this all over the hands and wipe off with a soft paper tissue or towel. All dirt will come away and leave the hands non-greasy, clean and smooth. The constant use of soap and water tends to increase the dryness.

MOIST HANDS. Moist hands are usually found in young people. It is often a form of nervousness and, although the sufferer may not be conscious of it, a nervous excitement makes the pores of the skin open and close and throw off moisture. The sufferer often grows completely out of this condition but, while it lasts, it is extremely unpleasant.

There is no actual cure but, an astringent lotion used several times a day, will greatly help the condition, and a good talcum powder applied two or three times a day will make the hands more comfortable. If you are going to a party take some astringent lotion or perfume in your hand-bag and use it at intervals to freshen your hands.

BAD CIRCULATION AND RED, SWOLLEN HANDS. The circulation of the hands is most important; bad circulation causes swelling, redness, numbness and many complaints of both hands and nails. General health, exercise, massage, and a fully developed nail are important factors if the circulation is to be kept normal. It is not generally realised how important the development of the nail is. A fully developed nail, with normal cuticles, the pink part of the nailplate well attached to the finger-tip, with well grooved sides, aids the circulation of the whole hand.

An easy and splendid stimulant, and one which will not

D

only improve the circulation but help the hands to remain youthful, is to brush the skin all over with a medium stiff brush. Do this for three or four minutes every day and until the skin tingles with warmth. Then apply a good cream to penetrate and nourish the skin. Another beneficial treatment for the circulation, redness and swelling, is to plunge the hands for twenty minutes into a bowl of hot water, to which add a handful of the following mixture:

$\frac{1}{3}$ water softener : $\frac{1}{3}$ kitchen salt : $\frac{1}{3}$ epsom salt.

Mix these all together and keep in a tin.

This treatment will open the pores and relieve the condition. Afterwards apply a good nourishing cream and wear gloves.

This treatment may be employed every day for two or three weeks – but if the skin becomes sensitive – every other day. These treatments should be augmented by deep hand massage, electric vibration, clay packs and hand wax baths.

CHILBLAINS. Chilblains are a condition of the blood and are sometimes an indication of a deficiency of calcium and poor circulation. The condition can be greatly helped by supplying the body with the deficiency, and a course of liquid calcium is very beneficial. This should be augmented by halibut oil and suitable ointments for exterior relief. A nourishing diet is necessary, with plenty of fresh air and exercise, while extremes of heat and cold should be avoided.

When chilblains are starting, raise the arms vertically and practise extension and flexion of the fingers several times a day. Massage the skin gently with camphorated oil if the skin is unbroken. If the condition becomes painful and the chilblains break it is better to consult a doctor. There are many chilblain remedies available but none are really effective without remedying the body deficiency and improving the circulation. Loose warm fur, or fur-lined gloves should be worn in cold weather.

ENLARGED KNUCKLES. Of all hand troubles enlarged knuckles are clearly the most disfiguring and difficult to manage. There are many causes for this unsightly condition, the worst being osteo-arthritis, for which there is no known cure. Amongst other causes of this trouble are acidity, rheumatism and long immersion in water or wet substances.

The following treatments will greatly alleviate the condition and the day should be planned so that fifteen minutes are available each night to carry out treatment.

Deep massage, wax baths, electric vibration, exercises, radiant heat, osteopathy, clay packs all help to eradicate this trouble – which is usually found in elderly people. Your doctor should be consulted for constitutional treatment.

Here is an excellent exercise for enlarged knuckles : Double all the fingers over so that the tips of the fingers are touching the phalange nearest the palm of the hand, then open up the fingers, stretch them out as far as possible and repeat this exercise for five minutes, several times a day. It will not be possible in many cases to touch the phalange nearest the palm because of stiffness and swelling, but the exercise consists in trying to do this.

Iodine X painted on the knuckles at night is often a help.

If the skin of the hands is dry as well, and cream and gloves are being worn, cut the fingers of the gloves off just above the knuckles, as creams often contain moisture. Dampness of any kind is bad for enlarged knuckles.

The salt bath treatment outlined in the chapter for bad circulation should be used every day and the hands frequently plunged into warm wax baths.

Keep the hands out of water and, above all, never strain the delicate bone structure of the hands and fingers. For example, do not take the weight of a heavy saucepan on your fingers. Take the weight with the palm and fingers of both hands because, if the bones of the fingers become displaced by the weight of the saucepan, rheumatism and arthritis can set in, and the displacement will cause tension in the whole hand and gradually will pull the hand completely out of alignment.

BROWN PATCHES AND FRECKLES. As the hands age, small brown patches, rather like freckles, appear on the back of the hand. There is no cure for these. Any substance which is strong enough to remove them will injure the skin and leave a white patch instead of a brown one.

A nourishing bleaching cream will lighten their colour and improve the skin generally. There are acids and rays which will remove them but in the case of freckles these will appear again on a new patch of skin, so all treatment other than a gentle bleaching should be discouraged.

WARTS. These disfiguring growths are best removed by a qualified practitioner. There are remedies supplied by the chemist but these are not always successful and when they fail – it is better to have expert treatment.

TO REMOVE STAINS HARMLESSLY. Stains on the hands caused by ink or iodine can be removed by a weak solution of ammonia and water, to which add lemon juice. Instructions for making this will be found under the heading Stain Remover (pp. 27–8). Nicotine stains are not easy to remove as a solution strong enough to remove the nicotine can damage the skin. Pumice stone is not injurious, and weak peroxide may be rubbed into the skin after using pumice stone.

Excessive Irritation of the Hands

Excessive irritation of the hands, sometimes accompanied by redness and swelling can be caused by eczema, dermatitis or occupation. The undermentioned treatment will alleviate it and stop the irritation. The following preparations are necessary for the treatment:

1 pair rubber gloves : 2 pairs cotton gloves (one pair ordinary size, one pair extra large size) : 1 bottle alcohol : 1 jar of calomine ointment : 1 jar of water base hand cream, such as Coralie's *Klenza* : 1 roll of cotton wool : 1 bowl of cold water : some soft tissues.

METHOD OF TREATMENT FOR IRRITATION OF THE HANDS.

1. Never allow the hands to come into contact with soap and water. Use rubber gloves over cotton ones for all

work and immersion in water. Wash and dry the inner cotton gloves frequently.

2. Wash the hands several times a day with alcohol. Should the alcohol sting dilute it with water until it feels comfortable. As the hands improve, gradually reduce the water until the alcohol is being used neat. Apply a minimum of calomine ointment all over after the alcohol and wipe the surplus away with soft tissues.

3. At night make sufficient pads of cotton wool to cover the irritating spots or, if necessary, the whole hand. Wet the cotton wool with cold water and press the surplus water away. Apply the alcohol to the hands then apply the calomine ointment liberally all over.

Put on the wet cotton pads and encase the hands in the extra large size gloves so that the pads are kept in position. Keep a bowl of cold water by the bedside and if the irritation starts again during the night wet the pads again in cold water. The wet pads will open the pores of the skin and take the irritation and inflammation away.

4. When the condition has cleared up always use alcohol as a hand lotion after washing the hands, and use a water base cream such as Coralie's *Klenza* after the alcohol.

5. On the slightest suggestion of a recurrence of the trouble revert to the original treatment.

6. As the skin improves, vigorously rub alcohol into the pores with cotton wool, twice a day, in addition to using alcohol as a hand lotion.

7. Heavy nourishing creams and glycerine should be avoided.

THIN HANDS. Very gentle massage with nourishing creams and oils are best for this condition. It is constitutional, and a fattening diet will best remedy the defect.

CRACKS AND SPLITS. Sometimes there are really stubborn cracks and splits of the skin which often appear at the finger-tips near the nail groove and which will not heal with ordinary nourishing creams or lotions. For cases such as these a reliable and safe formula is the following:

8 ozs. petroleum : 2 ozs. beeswax : 1 oz. benzoin :
4 ozs. gum thus : 4 ozs. olive oil : $\frac{1}{2}$ oz. cam-
phor : $\frac{1}{16}$ oz. oil of eucalyptus.

Mix all well together and apply freely at night and wear gloves.

The cracks should be rubbed down when dry (and before applying the cream) with an emery board.

SPECIAL CARE FOR GARDENING. Gardening is one of the worst occupations for destroying the hands; if the hands are not protected and extra care taken before, and after, gardening it can be a source of fungi infection. To avoid this proceed as follows:

Fill the nails with a greaseless water soluble cream such as *Klenza* and spread the cream all over the hands as well. Put on a thin pair of cotton gloves and over them a stout pair of gardening gloves. The stout outer gloves can be removed when seedlings and delicate plants need handling, but the outer gloves should be left on over the thin ones for all work which does not require a delicate touch. When the gardening is finished the water soluble cream can be removed by washing the hands. The soil and dirt will come away with it. The hands should then be finished with a nourishing cream. The thin inner pair of cotton gloves should be washed every time they are used and several pairs kept for use. The outer gloves need not be cleaned so often.

By keeping the inner pair of gloves clean only the minimum amount of dirt is absorbed by the hands and nails. This extra care considerably helps the hands and nails to withstand the damaging effects of gardening.

OCCUPATIONAL DISORDERS. There are many other occupations besides gardening which injure and destroy the health and beauty of the hands. Nurses, cooks, barmaids, factory workers and housewives – these are difficult occupations.

When the hands are in a bad condition no cure or im-

provement is possible until all wet and irritating substances
are completely avoided and protecting gloves worn for work.
With perseverance, care and, above all, protection, the hands
will recover and stand up to most occupations.

Sometimes, due to a long period of neglect or irritating.
substances being in constant contact with the hands, the
condition becomes serious and the skin infected. Then a
change of occupation may be necessary for full recovery.
The routine recommended for *dry hands* will be found the
best for general daily use.

MOVEMENTS FOR HAND MASSAGE. Hand massage
should be firm and the movements quick and stimulating.
Practise the movements slowly at first and when you know
them by heart speed them up and finish with a brisk friction
of the whole hand. You will need a suitable cream as a
massage medium. A water soluble cream such as *Klenza* is
best as it will easily wipe off and will not leave the hands
so oily as heavier creams. See that you have soft paper towels
and a spirit lotion ready to apply after massage (Plate 9a).

Massage the fingers.

1. Apply massage cream to the client's whole hand.
Then place the hand, palm downwards, facing you.

2. Start with the client's little finger and, with a circular
movement, massage the finger-tip – using the pad of
your thumb and first finger.

3. With a backward and forward movement massage
the knuckle, using the pad of your thumb. To do this,
grip the finger in your whole hand, with your thumb
uppermost. Now move your thumb from left to right
and right to left, backwards and forwards which will,
by this movement, massage the knuckle. Continue for
all fingers.

4. With a downward clasping movement massage the
whole finger, using all your fingers and thumb.

5. Repeat movements for each finger and thumb.

Massage the back of the hand.

1. With the client's hand palm downwards and facing

you, place your thumbs on the back of the hand and your eight fingers holding it underneath.

2. Using the pads of your two thumbs alternately, make short upward movements one after the other, all over the back of the hand up to the wrist. Massage gently over the veins as they are near the surface and care must be taken not to bruise them.

3. Holding the client's hand in the same position as movement 1 – give a general massage, using all your fingers, your thumbs, and the palms of your hands. Use both your hands, one after the other; make the movements circular.

4. Double up your first finger and use it with the pad of your thumb in a pinching movement to massage the flesh between the client's thumb and first finger.

Massage the palm of the hand. Rest the client's elbow on the table, the palm facing you, and using the same movements with the pads of your thumbs as on the back of the hands. Massage the palm all over.

Massage for improving the shape. With the client's elbow resting on the table, use both your hands exactly as if you were trying to put gloves on the client. Use downward strokes with one hand after the other, making the movements from finger-tips to wrist and clasping the client's whole hand in yours.

Friction of fingers. Replace the hand, palm downwards, facing you. Place your thumbs across your palms and close your other fingers over the thumbs. You now have two doubled-up fists (Plate 9b).

Now bring your two hands together so that your first fingers and thumbs meet. Place the client's outstretched finger between your doubled-up fists – go forward with your right fist and backward with the left fist, holding the finger firmly. Repeat this backward and forward movement many times on the finger until the flesh glows.

See that you give the friction with the flesh and not with the bones of your hand.

Repeat the movement on all the client's fingers, going backwards and forwards many times on each finger.

Finally. Complete the movements by giving an all-over general massage, using both your hands. Repeat all the movements from the beginning again. The hand massage should take from ten to fifteen minutes.

ELECTRIC VIBRO MASSAGE. Vibro massage penetrates deeply into the tissues and is beneficial to the circulation. When using the vibrator care should be taken to use it gently over the backs of the hands, as the veins can be easily bruised. This also applies when vibrating the feet. The vibrator should not be used over the instep. The veins lie nearer to the surface in these two parts of the body and easily bruise. See Plate 10.

To operate the vibrator. Place the client's hand palm downwards with the finger-tips facing you. Vibrate the fingers all over, avoiding the nails and cuticles which are too sensitive for vibration.

Now place the hand upright with the client's elbow on the table and palm facing you. Run the vibrator down each finger, starting at the tip of the finger, and bend each joint over the vibrator end as you come to it; then vibrate the palm all over several times.

After vibrating one hand ask the client to close and open both hands. A distinct difference will be felt: the hand which has been vibrated will feel soft and supple while the other hand will not feel this softness and suppleness.

Vibration may be used for a few minutes three or four times a day and is more necessary in winter than in summer.

HAND EXERCISES.

1. Stretch hands and fingers to their fullest extent, relax. Repeat movement 10 times.

2. Try to touch with all finger-tips at once the point at which the finger joins the palm. This will bend all the knuckles and stretch the palm of the hand. Repeat 10 times.

3. Shake hands vigorously from a loose wrist so that the

finger-tips touch each other at each shake. Repeat 10 times.

4. Hold hands together with fingers extended as if praying, and press the fingers as far as possible first to left and then right. Repeat 10 times.

WAX BATHS FOR THE HANDS. Wax baths for the hands, besides being enjoyable and comforting, are helpful for bad circulation, rheumatism, swelling, stiffness etc. They also nourish the nailplate and greatly improve discoloration of the free-edge of the nailplate, leaving it clear and a good colour. Wax baths may be used every day and are most beneficial.

A special electric hot plate is needed for melting the wax. It should be thermostatically controlled and capable of keeping the wax in a liquid state at a very low temperature. Consult an electrician and order an electric hot plate specially adapted. The wax should have a low melting point, to avoid burning the skin. Special waxes are made for this purpose.

You will also need large sheets of wax paper, two towels large enough to wrap up the hands; a minute 'timer', massage cream, vibrator, a small hair brush, paper tissues, hand lotion, powder, and other towels for general use. If no electric hot plate is available for melting the wax, a water bath will melt it. This consists of an outer pan containing hot water and an inner one containing the wax. A porringer makes a good water bath for melting purposes.

The wax should be only just melted and not at all hot. The temperature is at its best when the wax is seen to be setting round the edges of the bowl and the body of the wax is liquid. The bowl holding the wax should be stainless steel and it should be large enough to take 3 lbs. or 4 lbs. of wax, so that the hand can be fully immersed in the wax.

Before using the wax, test it on your own hand first so that there will be no possibility of it being too hot for the client.

When you have assembled all your requirements proceed as follows:

1. Brush one hand with the hair brush for approximately 1 minute, all over, to help the circulation.

2. Vibrate the hand for approximately 2 minutes (see Vibration).

3. Place the bowl of wax on the table and immerse the whole hand in it. Remove and keep the hand out of the bowl for a second to allow the wax to set. Repeat this five times.

Each time the coating of wax will get thicker. Finally, allow a few seconds for the wax to set on the hand.

4. Place a large sheet of wax paper on the table and put the hand now covered in wax, palm downwards, on this paper, and fold the paper so that the hand is completely covered up.

This helps to retain the heat of the wax. Now wrap up the waxed hand in a large warm towel and place the wrapped waxed hand out of the way on the side of the table.

5. Set your minute timer for 10 minutes.

6. Proceed with the other hand. Brush it for 1 minute, vibrate it 2 minutes and now, in addition, massage it (see Hand massage) for approximately 6 minutes; then wipe the massage cream off completely with paper tissues, to enable the skin to take the wax.

A water soluble cream such as *Klenza* is best.

Then proceed to wax and cover the hand as before. Next, place the covered hand out of the way on the side of the table. Your minute timer should now be re-set for another 10 minutes.

7. The other hand has now been enclosed in wax for 10 minutes. Remove the towel and wax paper. The wax on the hand should be lifted away at the wrist first and then, with a downward movement, the whole of the wax will come off like a glove.

Put the wax on one side to be dealt with later. Now give this hand 6 minutes massage. Completely remove the massage cream, apply olive or almond oil and rub in.

The hot wax bath opens the pores of the skin and the purpose of the olive oil or almond oil is to penetrate the skin and nourish it at a time when the skin is most receptive.

Finally, wipe the hand well to remove all trace of oil and, where desired, apply hand lotion and powder. With an orange stick gently remove the wax from underneath the free-edge of each nailplate.

8. Remove the towel, wax paper and wax from the other hand and finish in the same way as before. The treatment is now finished and the hands should look, and feel, much better.

By the end of the day you will have accumulated a large quantity of used wax. This can be sterilized by pouring boiling water on it and allowing it to set. When it has set and the water is cold – lift the wax away from the water – turn the wax over bottom side up and remove with a knife any debris which has collected on the underneath side of the wax. This scalding of the wax should be repeated and, where there is any abrasion of the skin in the hands being treated, the wax should be thrown away. The wax remaining in the bowl should also be cleaned in this way; and everything that you have used should be thoroughly cleaned. Hot water and soap will remove any spilt wax from clothes, floors or tables. A thin plastic cape or coat put on the client back to front will ensure that the wax does not touch her clothes.

CLAY PACK FOR THE HANDS. Many skin irritations, swellings, redness and roughness of the hands respond quickly to the soothing effect of clay packs. Buy a suitable clay at the chemist – kaolin is excellent – and mix it to a thick cream gradually, with water.

The following assortment of appliances and preparations are necessary for the treatment:

1 large roll of cotton wool. (Cover this with plastic, tie up at both ends and use as an arm rest) : 1 hand bowl warm water : 1 bottle almond or peach oil : 1 bottle hand lotion : 1 large square of plastic material : 1 hand

bowl of mixed clay : 1 empty hand bowl : 1 cake of
super-fatted soap : 1 large plastic cape or coat : 1 jar
massage cream : towels and soft tissues.

Method of applying clay pack to the hands.
1. Place the plastic coat on the client back to front to
avoid any of the clay spoiling her clothes.
2. Spread the plastic material all over the table.
3. Immerse one hand in the bowl of clay and leave it
there for a few seconds. Then remove the hand and
place the wrist and arm on the arm rest so that the
hand hangs over the rest. Leave it resting on one side of
the table so that it is not in the way, the surplus clay
dripping into the empty bowl.
4. Massage the other hand for ten minutes, wash the
massage cream off with soap and water, dry the hand
and immerse it in the bowl of clay.
   If the hand is not washed with soap and water, and
well dried, the clay will not adhere to it.
5. Remove the arm rest and empty hand bowl from the
other wrist and arm and place them under the wrist
and arm of the hand which has been massaged and
dipped into the clay.
   See that the arm rests comfortably and the surplus
clay drips in the bowl.
6. Wash the clay off the first hand, well dry it, and
massage for ten minutes.
7. Wash both hands free of clay and massage cream.
Well dry them and massage the oil in all over. Remove
the surplus oil with soft tissues. Wash the hands again,
if desired, and apply the hand lotion, and wipe the
hands well.
An electric vibrator is a good finish for this treatment. It
makes the hands supple and improves the circulation of the
whole hand.
GROOMING A MAN'S HANDS. The faults in a man's
hand cannot be disguised in the same way as in the hands

of a woman because a man does not use any artifices to hide
the defects caused by wear and tear. A man's hands usually
show very clearly his occupation and hobbies and there is
a vast difference in the hands of a man who does manual
work and one who does not. A woman can cover over the
blemishes caused by housework or other tasks by cream and
powder plus nail enamel, but a man has no such aids to
cover up the blemishes caused by his work. It is easier with
sedentary occupations because here the hands do not become
calloused and hard so, where the hands are not rough or
hard, proceed as follows:

Wash the hands in warm water and dry them very well.
The nails should have the corners well embedded in the
finger-tip. Do not shape the nail to a point or an exaggerated
oval; shape it to harmonise with the contour of the finger-
tip. The nail should not be shorter than the finger-tip. Define
the half moon by pressing gently with a rubber-ended hoof
stick. To keep the surface of the nail shiny it can be rubbed
with a chamois leather.

When the hands are calloused and used for manual work,
rub the callouses away with the soft side of an emery board:
a little every day, and remove cigarette stains with pumice
stone; keep the nails short and square.

There are several good hand cleansers on the market and,
where necessary, one of these should be used in addition to
soap and water. The last wash every night should be followed
by a good emolient cream well rubbed in all over the hands
– and the surplus wiped away with a towel or paper tissues.

A professional manicure at regular intervals will be a great
help, but do not allow the manicurist to file the corners of
the nail away, cut the cuticle, or dig into the free-edge of the
nailplate.

JEWELLERY AND HANDS. When choosing jewellery such
as rings and bracelets, the age, shape of the hand and suit-
ability of the jewellery should be considered. Very large
stones and heavy, old-fashioned rings are not attractive on
the very young. A well-shaped hand can take almost any

type of ring and it will look beautiful, but a fat, plump hand would do well to choose oblong or marquise shaped rings.

An engagement, wedding and signet ring are usual, and quality is more important than quantity where jewellery is concerned. When there is some serious defect of hands or nails, rings will draw attention to the defect and it is better to dispense with them altogether or wear the minimum possible.

A ring should slip with ease over the knuckle of the finger as, constantly forcing a tight fitting ring over the knuckle will, in time, cause hard skin, enlarge the knuckle and distort the shape of the finger.

Bracelets and watches are more flattering to the hand when worn about two inches above the wrist. This position gives the hand a more slender appearance, whereas a bracelet or watch worn on the wrist itself foreshortens the distance between the wrist and the finger-tips and, in the case of plump hands, is especially unattractive.

GOING TO A PARTY. So often one is invited to an unexpected party and, although there may be a lovely dress to wear, perhaps just that day, one's hands and nails look their worst and there is no time for a professional manicure.

The hands and nails can be greatly improved and rendered attractive by a simple home treatment which will obliterate the ravages caused by the many uses to which we subject our hands and nails.

First, make a bleach pack for the hands with almond meal or kaolin mixed to a thick creamy texture with water. Plunge both hands in this and allow them to remain in the bleach pack for about ten or fifteen minutes. This will whiten the hands and improve the texture of the skin. Next wash the hands in warm water and super-fatted soap. Well dry them and apply a hand cream or lotion.

After the hand cream well powder the hands with a near-white powder. Next, clean the free-edge of the nails and cuticles with lemon juice and apply a nail enamel to match your dress. Allow plenty of time for the enamel to dry and finish with some of your favourite perfume on the palm of the hand. If you want your hands to look their best during the party – keep the hands and arms turned upwards from the elbows when it is possible to do so without drawing attention to the fact.

The position for the hands to look their best can be clearly seen in the frontispiece.

RECIPE FOR HAND CREAM. A recipe for making a a nourishing hand cream is useful to most women and the following cream is designed for use at night and can be used either with gloves, or without. It is not suitable for day use, special occasions, or where the hands are in need of specialized treatment, when it is better to buy day creams and skin deficiency preparations from reputable manufacturers.

For the nourishing hand cream, buy from your chemist:

2 ozs. lanolin : 2 ozs. white petroleum : 2 ozs. cold cream : 2 ozs. almond oil;

mix these all together with a wooden spoon. The mixing will be easier if you put them all together in a basin and place the basin over a saucepan of hot water. The mixture should be beaten to a creamy consistency and extra almond oil added if necessary. The finished cream should be potted into screw-top jars and labelled. Some perfume may be added if desired. This hand cream is excellent for dry and rough hands.

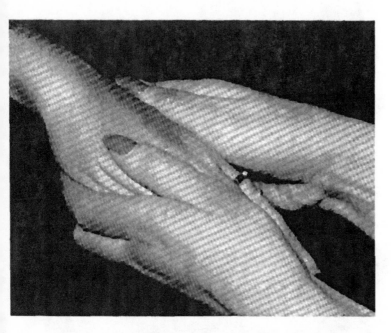

9a   Massaging the hand (movement 1)

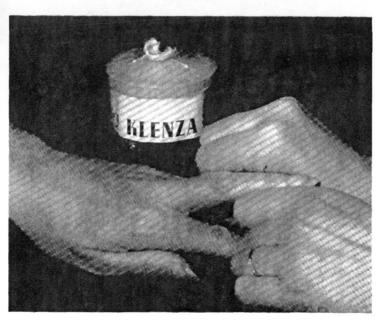

9b   Friction of the fingers

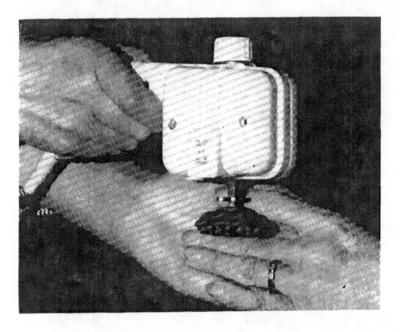

10   Vibrating the fingers

4

PEDICURE

Pedicure is giving the same attention to the toe-nails and feet that is given to the hands and finger-nails. Foot care is an essential part of the well-groomed man or woman.

The general treatment is almost the same as for hands but there are several deviations when treating the toe-nails which should be strictly adhered to, as the toe-nails are usually more sensitive than the finger-nails, and allowance must be made for this. Pedicure, with foot massage, should be an enjoyable, relaxing experience and the clients should feel that their feet are several sizes smaller than before the pedicure began. In fact, a pedicure, with foot massage, should give that 'walking on air' feeling.

Pedicure can, in no way, replace the skilled attention of a qualified chiropodist and a chiropodist should be consulted for corns, verrucapedis, inflammatory conditions of the feet and other disorders which cause discomfort.

METHOD OF PEDICURE.

1. Place the client in a comfortable reclining chair with a leg extension, and have a small stool for yourself. See that the stool is not too high, so that your back is saved undue strain in bending over.

2. Remove the shoes and stockings and start by giving the feet an all-over friction with a good lotion containing spirit – a toilet water is excellent.

3. Remove nail enamel (if any) from the toe-nails.

4. With the coarse side of an emery board, or corn rasp, file down all the hard skin and corns.

5. Clip the toe-nails to length, using nail clippers. Sometimes the toe-nails are very thick and hard, and the clipping will have to be done by taking away small pieces of nail at a time; gradually clipping away small pieces of nail until the correct length has been obtained.

Do not make the toe-nail shorter than the flesh at the tip of the toe. The toe-nail should be level with the toe itself and should be clipped straight across and not shaped like a finger-nail.

Leave the sides of the toe-nail well on. It is possible to buy a small type of nail clipper which is lighter in weight and easier to manipulate on a toe-nail.

6. Filing is done with an emery board and not a steel file. It is important that the edge of the emery board does not touch the toe as the toe pad is extremely sensitive.

To avoid this, put the flat side of the emery board on the edge of the toe-nail and run the emery board in downward strokes, gently, without touching the toe pad. See Plate 11.

Continue these downward light strokes until the edge of the toe-nail is smooth and even.

7. Disinfect the cuticles and proceed as you would for finger-nails, but using more delicate movements and avoiding the use of instruments wherever the cuticle is inflamed.

Some cuticles are so sensitive that a gentle clean-up with a rubber-ended hoof stick and disinfectant is all that should be done to the cuticle.

8. With an orange stick and disinfectant gently clean underneath the free-edge of the nailplate and round the nail groove.

9. Massage the feet with a water soluble cream such as *Klenza*, for twenty to thirty minutes, as fully explained in the section on Foot Massage which follows.

10. Remove the cream with a soft towel and well friction the feet with a spirit lotion.

11. Using an electric vibrator – the soles of the feet may be vibrated for two or three minutes. Do not vibrate the instep because the veins are too near the surface.

12. Well powder the feet, especially between the toes.

13. Place pads of cotton wool between all the toes, to separate them and prevent them coming into contact with nail enamel, and apply nail enamel of the desired shade. See Plate 12a.

Allow plenty of time for the enamel to dry. If the enamel is not dry it will stick to the stockings and make holes in them.

A small electric hand dryer is useful to speed up the drying. The cold air of the dryer should be used and not the hot air.

FOOT MASSAGE.

1. Cream each toe separately, starting with the little toe, using a general rotary downward movement, then cream the whole foot.

2. Place the foot in an upright position with the heel resting on your lap and massage each toe pad upwards with the thumbs, using one thumb after the other in quick successive upward movements.

The four fingers of each hand should be resting on the instep of the foot whilst doing these movements.

3. Massage the pad of the foot with the thumbs in the same way as in number 2, using downward movements, firmly pressing the pad of the foot well in.

Continue this movement downwards the whole length of the foot from pads of the toes to the heel.

4. With the foot still upright and the heel resting on your lap, enter into a general movement: thumbs on the sole of the foot, fingers and palms of hands on instep – massage up and down without removing the hands from the foot, with great pressure on the sole of

the foot on the downward movement, and coming up lightly.

This general movement, which is very soothing, should be used between all the movements from 1 to 12, so that during a foot massage this movement takes place twelve times.

5. Place the first finger of your hand so that it separates the big toe from the other toes.

Make a fist of your other hand, with your thumb inside, across your palm, and massage the big toe joint up and down with the thumb cushion of your hand, with great pressure on the downward movement as in Plate 12b.

6. Remove your first finger and massage the pad of the foot with this same movement, holding the foot with your right hand and massaging the pad of the foot with the left hand.

7. Bend the toes towards you and cup the hands, placing the thumbs on the instep of the foot and use rotating massage movements with both hands – massaging in this way all over the top and bottom of the foot as in Plate 13.

8. Place the foot in an upright position, with the heel on your lap, and with the pads of your thumb on the sole of the foot, one above the other, massage, with crosswise movements, the complete sole up and down, with the fingers of your hand resting on the instep of the client's foot.

9. Hold the foot with your left hand and massage the heel with the palm and fingers of your right hand, using a circular movement – then, with your fingers doubled over, use your thumb and doubled over first finger to knead the hard skin round the heel.

10. Using one hand after the other with circular upward movements: massage the flesh round the back of the ankle, then, continue with circular, sweeping movements, upwards towards the calf.

11. With the palms and fingers of both your hands massage with a rotary movement the ankle and instep.

12. Place one palm after the other on the instep of the foot and massage upwards; then massage, with long sweeping movements from toes to above the ankle.

Foot massage should take approximately 20 to 30 minutes and during that time the whole series of movements can be repeated two or three times.

WAX BATHS FOR THE FEET. This treatment will be found a boon in cold weather. It will improve the circulation, reduce swelling, improve the skin and toe-nails and make the feet feel warm and comfortable.

Wax baths for the feet can be used every day, if desired, with beneficial results. Full details for buying and melting the wax will be found in the Chapter on HANDS, but for the feet the method is slightly different.

The following equipment is necessary for the treatment, and the wax must be much cooler than when it is used for the hands:

1 large bowl of luke warm wax : 1 large piece of plastic material : 2 large squares of waxed paper : 3 large turkish towels : 1 jar of massage cream : 1 bottle of almond or olive oil : 1 bottle toilet water : 1 box foot powder : some soft tissues.

Method of applying wax to the feet.

1. Spread the large piece of plastic material all over the floor. Any spilt wax can easily be washed off afterwards with hot water and soap.

2. Place the client in a comfortable chair, with one leg on a leg rest and the foot of the other leg in the bowl of warm wax on the floor.

3. Dip the foot in and out of the wax three times, allowing a short period each time for the wax to set on the foot.

4. When the wax has set in a thick coating on the foot, remove the bowl from underneath and wrap the foot up in a large square of waxed paper.

The waxed paper must be large enough to cover all the wax on the foot. Then take one of the large turkish towels and wrap the foot up in it, so that it completely covers over the waxed paper and the towel looks like a large bootee. This will keep the wax warm and enclosed. Place this wrapped foot on a leg rest.

5. Massage the other foot for ten minutes. Remove the massage cream with tissues first and finish with a towel; then apply the wax in the same way as before.

6. Remove the wax from the first foot and massage for ten minutes.

7. Remove all the wax and cream from both feet. Massage the oil well in all over the feet and remove the surplus with soft paper tissues, friction the feet with toilet water, well dry them especially between the toes and apply foot powder liberally.

CLAY PACKS FOR THE FEET. In hot weather there is nothing more soothing or refreshing to the feet than a clay pack. The clay reduces any swelling and has a healing effect on the skin. For tired, aching and troublesome feet it is most beneficial. The clay pack treatment can be applied two or three times a week, or more, if desired.

Most chemists and health food stores sell clay suitable for packs, and kaolin is excellent. It comes in powder form and should gradually be mixed to a thick cream, with water. The following assortment of appliances and preparations are necessary for the treatment:

2 small plastic trays : 1 two inch soft paint brush : 1 large bowl of warm water : 1 bottle of almond, peach, or olive oil : 1 bottle toilet water : 2 turkish towels : 1 box foot powder : 1 large piece plastic material : 1 jar of massage cream : 1 cake of soap : some soft tissues.

Method of applying clay pack to the feet.

1. Spread the large piece of plastic material all over the floor because any spilt clay will be easier to clear up afterwards.

2. Place the client in a comfortable chair, with one leg

on a leg rest and the foot of the other leg resting on a
plastic tray on the floor. Brush this foot and ankle
liberally all over with the clay and leave the foot on
the tray.

3. Massage the other foot for ten minutes; after the
massage wash the foot in the large bowl of warm water,
well dry it, and brush the foot and ankle all over with
the clay and leave it on the floor.

4. Wash the clay off the other foot with soap and water,
well dry it, place the leg on the leg rest and massage the
foot for ten minutes.

5. Wash both feet, well dry them, and massage the oil
in all over. Remove the surplus oil with soft paper
tissues.

6. Friction the feet with toilet water and well dry them,
especially between the toes.

7. Apply foot powder liberally.

TREATMENT FOR TROUBLESOME FEET. Feet which
excessively perspire, especially between the toes, can be
helped by regular treatment at home. The treatment should
be carried out night and morning to keep them in a healthy
condition and can be carried out several times a day, with
beneficial results, when the condition is very bad. As the
condition improves reduce the number of treatments a day
until only one or two a day are necessary.

1. Wash the feet in luke warm, not hot, water and, if
possible, rinse them in cold water and well dry them.

2. Liberally apply pure alcohol all over them and allow
to dry. If there is much inflammation dilute the alcohol
with a little water. When the condition improves always
use neat alcohol.

3. Where there is any inflammation dab on a little
calomine lotion or ointment, whichever suits the
skin best.

4. Be sure the feet are perfectly dry, especially between
the toes, and heavily powder them with an anti-fungus
foot powder, using it generously between the toes.

5. Place a small wisp of lambs wool (not cotton wool) between each toe.

6. Change your stockings or socks and shoes every day and keep all the shoes which are not being worn in the fresh air. Do not put them away in a cupboard.

Fit your shoes with lightweight inner soles and change them frequently. Wear no socks or stockings at home and use sandals as much as possible so that the air can get to the feet.

7. Where there is an offensive odour to the feet, in addition to the foregoing, the shoes should be lightly brushed inside once a month with formaldehyde powder. It should be left on for a few hours and wiped completely off the leather with a soft rag tied to a stick.

Do not allow this powder to come into contact with the hands or skin. It will burn the skin. Use rubber gloves when applying or removing it.

Formaldehyde is a strong and effective germicide for leather. Keep it well out of the reach of children.

ONYCHIA AND RINGWORM OF THE FEET. When the toe-nails are discoloured or look eaten away, this is usually caused by an infection. The full treatment advised in the chapter on Nail Disorders should be carried out as well as the above treatment.

INGROWING TOE-NAILS. This condition can cause great pain and discomfort and is often the result of the sides of the toe-nail being cut or filed away too much. The nail is always trying to regain its original form and as it grows it cuts into the flesh and the condition becomes worse each time the nailplate is cut away at the side.

To alleviate the condition and gradually to allow the nail-plate to return to its normal groove, thin wisps of lambs wool, saturated with castor or olive oil, should be wedged between the new growing nail and the flesh of the toe. If these thin wisps of oil-saturated lambs wool are kept permanently between the nail and the flesh of the toe the nail cannot ingrow and cause inflammation and pain.

When the toe-nail has regained its square shape and the sides of the nailplate are completely grown up again to the top of the toe, then the toe-nails should be kept short and square, but never shorter than a fraction from the tip of the toe, and the corners of the nailplate should not be cut or filed away.

If there is much inflammation or pain, apply compresses and preparations as fully detailed in the treatment for paronychia. Avoid tight stockings and shoes and give the feet as much freedom as possible.

5

TRAINING

There are not many centres where manicure is taught at the present time and if, after perusing the foregoing chapters, the student wishes to take professional advice and lessons, she will find that most manicure courses designed by the Hairdressing and Beauty trade are simply an additional subject useful to learn perhaps so that the client may have a manicure at the same time as her hair is being dressed or her beauty being attended to, but are totally inadequate where it is desired to specialise in hand and nail culture.

The serious student who wishes to place scientific hand and nail culture on a professional basis and who wishes to make a study of nail irregularities and infections will require more than is available at the beauty and hairdressing schools.

The course of lessons outlined in this chapter have been in use for many years at the Hand and Nail Culture Institute and have proved a successful curriculum for students. The lessons are divided into 24 sessions. The *theoretical* portion of the lesson should be studied and written down first and then the *practical* side undertaken. The students should practise several hours a day after the lesson, on models, and frequent revision of the theoretical and practical will be found necessary. The lessons all link up with the contents of this Manual and reference should be made to the list of Contents where the subject titles for each lesson will be found. The lessons embrace treatment for normal hands and nails and include a few lessons on irregularities of the nails.

For a beginner to become moderately efficient as a manicurist, six to twelve months can be considered an average time. For an experienced manicurist the Institute found one or two months necessary to learn the elementals of this particular method of nail culture. In this limited time the student will not go beyond Lesson 12.

An examination should be taken at the end of the training and a certificate given in accordance with the pupil's ability.

To extend this course the student should study and practise giving wax baths, clay packs and vibro massage.

The study of nail infections would take from six to twelve months longer before the manicurist would be capable of undertaking treatment.

The results obtained by the treatment of nail infections are a reward in themselves and well worth the extra study.

In time, no doubt, expert and experienced teachers will open schools and train students exclusively in the care of hands and nails, but until such time, the student can, if she wishes, apply to the Hand and Nail Culture Institute of 35, Old Bond Street, London, W.1, for training.

The Institute takes a limited number of students. These are divided into two classes. One course is designed for manicurists who are already practicing and wish to extend their knowledge, and another course is for novices. Practical and helpful advice will be given to anyone applying to the Institute.

It is often the young attractive girl who decides to take up manicure as a profession, thinking it requires only a few weeks tuition and can be easily learned. Nothing can be further from the truth as, after years of experience, new types of nail troubles constantly appear and one never really stops learning.

As this profession aims at beautifying and maintaining the nails in a healthy condition the appearance, personal cleanliness and disposition of the manicurist are of the utmost importance. The manicurist should always be neatly

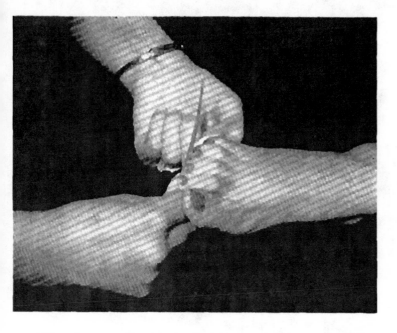

11　Filing the toe-nails with the flat side of an emery board

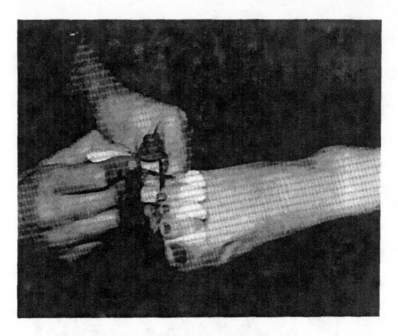

12a Applying nail enamel

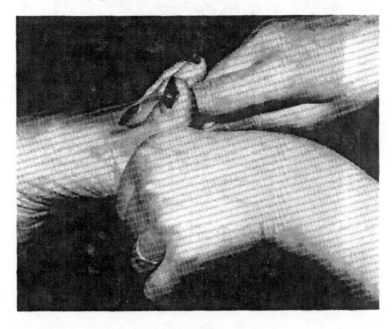

12b Massaging the joint of the big toe (movement 5)

attired in a clean, attractive overall; her hair should be well-groomed and her hands and nails spotless. Her disposition would best be described as someone who really enjoys doing things for others and making them happy.

Given these attributes the work is most compensating, for one sees beauty and health appear where there was ugliness and discomfort.

The Manicure Trousseau

One pair of Nail Clippers. These are specially curved with an inward sweep at the cutting edge. All clippers should have the spring released permanently to save strain. When the edges become blunt they can be re-sharpened by the suppliers. The best quality clippers should be used; inferior quality are not accurate. The clippers should have an edge which will scrape a nailplate effectively.

One pair of Cuticle Clippers. These are specially curved with an outward sweep at the cutting edge and should cut and trim with precision.

One Trimmer. A specially designed instrument for lifting the cuticles; it should be four inches long and chromium plated.

One pair of small straight-edge Scissors. Used to remove, by means of their blade, the top layer of the nailplate.

One Nail File. Should be six to eight inches long and unplated, as this is less harsh on the nail. This should be triple cut and flexible.

Six Emery boards. These should be tapered, with one fine and one coarse side. They should be about four inches long.

Six Orange Sticks. These should be four to five inches long.

Two Nail Polishers. These should be large, with detachable chamois leathers, which are washable. Two polishers are necessary: one for applying the polishing medium and one for finishing.

Six Chamois leathers. Cut in suitable sizes to fit the polishers. The leathers should be frequently washed.

Nail Polishing stone or powder. A good quality is essential;

F

well rub the chamois with the polishing medium, ready to polish the nails.

Hoof-stick. A shaped stick made of wood, bone, or plastic with a rubber hoof at one end and a point at the other, used to gently ease back the cuticle without injuring the embryo nail.

Electric Vibrator. With rubber pads for massaging and improving the circulation. Use a good quality vibrator as a weak machine will not stand up to constant use.

Small electric dryer. This is used to expedite the drying of nail enamel and is optional.

Cuticle disinfectant. Is easily made by dissolving ½ oz soft soap in one pint of hot water. Allow this to cool, add 4 ozs of alcohol and a little mild disinfectant; label and store in a screw-top bottle.

Liquid enamel remover. Should be a good quality non-acetone preparation and should contain oil.

Stain remover. A liquid preparation used to remove ink and iodine stains and clean under the free-edge of the nails.

Nicotine remover. A liquid preparation used to remove recent nicotine stains.

Pumice stone. This will be useful for deep-seated nicotine stains.

Iodine (brown). A useful addition for cuts and treatment.

Pheripa chloride. Stops bleeding.

Fine cotton wool. This is used to wrap round the tip of orange sticks.

Coarse cotton wool. Will be found useful for all other purposes.

Super-fatted soap. This is superior for cleansing hands and nails.

Cup-shaped sponge. The sponge should be approximately the size of a closed hand. It is used to clean hands and nails.

Alcohol. This is necessary to clean instruments and for use in treatments.

Healskin or Collodion. Useful for cuts and cracks of the cuticle.

Towels. The turkish type are best; they are more absorbent. Paper towels and soft paper tissues will be found a useful addition to turkish towels.

Glass tray. This should be about 8 by 6 inches, large enough to hold the manicure instruments, small bottles and jars.

Bottle of mild disinfectant. A few drops of the disinfectant should be used when washing the hands and manicure instruments.

Hand cream. A light type of cream suitable for use after washing the hands.

Massage cream. A water soluble base is best for hand and foot massage, such as *Klenza*.

Hand lotion. Hand powder, nail enamel various shades, nail and cuticle emolient (such as Healthinale).

Magnifying glass. This is useful to determine irregularities and infections.

CLEANING AND DISINFECTING INSTRUMENTS AND APPLIANCES. Manicure instruments which are not thoroughly disinfected can often be the means of carrying infection not only from one person to another but from one nail to the next.

All manicure instruments should be cleaned with alcohol before and after use. Make a small pad of cotton wool to apply the alcohol and rub the instrument all over, giving special attention to the cutting edges of the clippers. Orange sticks can be cleaned by rubbing their surface all over with an emery board and finishing with alcohol. Pots and jars are best cleaned with soap and water to which a few drops of disinfectant can be added. The tops and brushes of nail enamel bottles can be cleaned with a pad of cotton wool soaked in enamel remover.

The manicurist's hand should be frequently washed with soap and water to which a mild disinfectant has been added and the glass top of the treatment table should be kept hygienic and clean.

Clean towels should be used for each treatment and all appliances kept in an hygienic condition.

Lessons 1 to 24

LESSON 1. PREPARATION.

Theory. Study and write instructions for the Manicure Trousseau.

Practice. Make a small quantity of cuticle disinfectant using the formula given in the Manicure Trousseau.

The students should then receive a demonstration treatment and instructions for their own hands and nails. An exercise book will be necessary to write down the lessons, so that, at the end of the Course, there is a written record for their future guidance.

LESSON 2. HAND MASSAGE.

Theory. Study and write instructions for cleaning, disinfecting instruments and appliances, remover for nail enamel, stain remover, simple terms used in manicure, Chapter 3 on Hands, and movements for hand massage.

Practice. Hand massage. The use of stain remover, enamel remover and cuticle disinfectant.

LESSON 3. CLIPPING THE NAILS.

Theory. Study and write instructions for: the perfect nail, how nails are formed, the circulation of the nails, the effect of bad manicuring, the embryo nail, the dividing line and clipping the nailplate.

Practice. Clipping the nailplate with narrow strips of magazine paper. Hand massage.

LESSON 4. FILING THE NAILS.

Theory. Study and write instructions for filing and shaping the nailplate.

Practice. Filing the nailplate with a steel file and emery board, also shaping, clipping and hand massage.

LESSON 5. USING THE TRIMMER.

Theory. Study and write instructions for the cuticle, including acidity, rheumatism, unscientific cutting, liquid acid removers, lack of natural oil, how the cuticle sticks to the nail, how the cuticle influences the shape of the nail, types of cuticles, permanent diminishing, and lifting the cuticle with a trimmer.

Practice. Lifting the cuticle with a trimmer, disinfecting the cuticle, hand massage, clipping and filing the nailplate.

LESSON 6. SCRAPING UNDER CUTICLES.

Theory. Study and write instructions for scraping under the cuticles.

Practice. Scraping under the cuticles, clipping, filing and shaping the nailplate, and hand massage.

Note. Mix 2 ozs. ordinary flour with a little water into a stiff dough; store in a screw top jar ready for the next lesson.

LESSON 7. TRIMMING THE CUTICLES.

Theory. Study and write instructions for trimming and cutting the cuticles, splits and cracks of the cuticle, allowing the cuticle to stick to the nail, dry method, wet method.

Practice. Trimming and cutting cuticles by the following method:

Flatten a small piece of dough which was made during the last lesson, to the thickness of a cuticle, place in a 1 inch paper clip, leave about quarter of an inch edge of the dough beyond the clip and practise clipping small pieces of the dough away with the cuticle clippers. Later, practise taking a complete narrow rim away in one piece with the cuticle clippers. Practise clipping, filing and shaping the nailplate, clearing the cuticle, and hand massage.

LESSON 8. STRETCHING CUTICLES.

Theory. Study and write instructions for stretching the cuticles. The student cannot be told too often that stretching and cutting applies to thick, stubborn and growing cuticles.

To stretch or cut a normal, fine cuticle will result in hangnails, inflammation and further cuticle trouble.

Practice. Stretching the cuticles. With a suitable flat

piece of dough, held in a paper clip, practise stretching the dough with the cuticle clippers without cutting the dough. Practise clipping and filing the nailplate, clearing the cuticles, and hand massage.

LESSON 9. POLISHING.

Theory. Study and write instructions for polishing the nailplate and applying nail enamel.

Practice. Polishing the nailplate with a buffer, applying nail enamel, removing nail enamel, clipping and filing the nailplate, clearing the cuticles, and hand massage.

LESSON 10. PERSISTENT ADHERENCE.

Theory. Study and write instructions for persistent adherence of cuticles.

Practice. Treatment for persistent adherence. Lift and clear the cuticles, soak for a short time in warm water, dry the cuticles and finally run clear enamel underneath them.

While the enamel is drying the hands and fingers should be kept in an upright position so that the enamel remains under the cuticle. When the enamel is dry, remove any remaining on the nailplate.

Practise buffing the nailplate, applying nail enamel, and hand massage.

LESSON 11. CLEARING THE NAILPLATE.

Theory. Write instructions for clearing the nailplate of discoloration.

Practice. Treatment for clearing the nailplate. In cases where there is a slight yellow tinge or acidity – remove the top surface as directed. Soak the nails for five to ten minutes in hot water. Apply Iodine X all over the nails and allow it to dry.

This should be done late afternoon or evening and the hands should not be washed until the following morning.

Use a nail food after washing the hands the next morning. The brown Iodine X stains will disappear on washing the hands. Practise hand massage.

LESSON 12. METHOD OF MANICURE.
Theory. Revise from Lesson 1 to 10. Study and write instructions for Manicure Routine and Daily Routine.
Practice. The Manicure Routine and Daily Routine.

LESSON 13. BREAKING NAILS; TROUBLESOME CUTICLES.
Theory. Study and write instructions for Breaking nails and Troublesome cuticles.
Practice. The Manicure Routine.

LESSON 14. NAIL IRREGULARITIES.
Theory. Study and write instructions for Ridges, Biting the nails, White spots.
Practice. Treatment for Ridges. The Manicure Routine.

LESSON 15. PEDICURE.
Theory. Study and write instructions for Pedicure.
Practice. The Students receive a pedicure and instruction for their own toe-nails.

LESSON 16. FOOT MASSAGE.
Theory. Study and write instructions for Foot Massage.
Practice. Foot Massage.

LESSON 17. METHOD OF PEDICURE.
Theory. Study and write instructions for Method of Pedicure.
Practice. Method of Pedicure.

LESSON 18. REVISION.
Theory. Revise chapter on Nails and Cuticles.
Practice. Foot massage. Applying nail enamel to the toe-nails.

LESSON 19. REVISION.
Pedicure Routine on model.

LESSON 20. REVISION.
Manicure Routine on model.

LESSON 21. REVISION. Combined Manicure and Pedicure Routine on model.

LESSON 22. Student's own choice.

LESSON 23. Examination.

LESSON 24. Diploma.

When the Course and Examination have been satisfactorily completed the Student should be given a diploma and advice about using her knowledge to the best advantage.

There are Trade, Hairdressing and Beauty publications which always contain a list of vacant positions, or the Manicurist may prefer to work in a large factory as part of the Welfare Staff and, after a period of experience, perhaps open her own business. The Teacher should advise and help on these problems and the Student should feel that she can always rely on the guidance and support of her Teacher in her chosen career.

Manicure Routine

1. Remove nail enamel, apply nail emolient and wipe nailplate clean with cotton wool.
2. Clip nails to length and shape.
3. Shape with a file and finish with an emery board.
4. Disinfect cuticle.
5. Release and clear cuticle.
6. Apply cuticle emolient.
7. Massage hands.
8. Remove all cream and apply lotion and powder.
9. Clean round cuticle and free-edge of the nailplate with a cleaning fluid.
10. Wipe nailplate perfectly clean and polish with a buffer or apply nail enamel.

Daily Routine

To maintain healthy hands and nails.
1. Wash the hands as little as possible. After washing always apply a good hand cream or lotion to counteract the damaging effects of water.
2. Use gloves for all wet and dry work.
3. Never push the cuticles back with a towel after washing. This causes hangnails, redness, inflammation, and can result in infection.
4. Once or twice a day clear the cuticle and keep it lifted away from the nail by applying a cuticle emolient with

a rubber-ended hoof stick. Do not use acid cuticle removers.

5. Never cut or file away the corners of the nail. This distorts the shape of the nailplate, causes hard skin at the corners, makes the nailplate a flat and splay shape and causes many nail troubles.

6. Never dig into the free-edge of the nailplate when cleaning. This separates the nailplate from the finger.

Examination

1. Outline the Daily Routine.

2. State the causes for the nails being a bad shape. How can this be corrected?

3. Give two reasons for troublesome cuticles, and state why cuticles grow.

4. Describe the treatment necessary to permanently diminish the cuticle.

5. State all you know about the formation of the nail.

6. How would you clean a discoloured nailplate?

7. What treatment would you give for cuticles which persistently adhere to the nailplate?

8. How does the treatment of the nailplate differ in Manicure and Pedicure?

9. Describe the embryo nail.

10. What is the average rate of growth of the nail?

11. Describe a perfect nail.

12. Why are some injuries to the nailplate permanent and some temporary?

13. What is meant by the dividing line?

14. Draw a simple outline of a nail and name each part.

15. Is it better to clip or file the nails to length?

16. What are the three most important rules for healthy nails?

17. Why is a nail pink?

18. Give briefly the order of the Manicure Routine.

19. What is the function of the cuticle?

20. What corrective treatment is required on a thick cuticle?

21. Give the causes and treatment for breaking nails.

22. Give the causes and treatment for Ridges.

23. What treatment would you give for white spots on the nailplate?

24. Write out the treatment for people who bite their nails.

Opening a Salon

Many Students of this manual will wish to open their own Salon. Careful planning plus good management are essential to a successful business and the Student would be well advised to work first for two or three years as an Assistant in an establishment of high standards.

With this experience it is easier to train and retain one's own staff.

The experienced gained will also prevent financial loss.

When planning to open a Salon the first consideration is location so that the Clientele will have easy access to the premises.

The Salon should be light and airy, with plenty of windows and no dark corners.

Having chosen the Salon, a lease of several years should be acquired and a solicitor consulted with regard to its contents.

The whole Salon should then be painted in any pastel shades that appeal to the owner, bearing in mind that high gloss painted walls, although expensive at the beginning, are eventually the most economical, as every year, for at least six years, they can be washed down.

When walls are in a light pastel shade the furniture can be white or chromium, in either wood or metal. Metal furniture will be found more practical and durable in the long run. All this light, white or chromium furniture will give a pleasant, refreshing and hygienic appearance.

When it is desired to use colours of brilliant or deep tones, these are best employed in curtains and cushions.

The furniture should be practical, attractive and comfortable.

A visit should be made to the special firms who cater for Salon equipment. Their addresses can be found in the Trade Journals.

The premises should be divided up so that there are several cubicles for treatment, a Reception Salon, an office, and a room exclusively for staff. The latter should be cheerful, bright and airy, with facilities for making a light meal and an abundant supply of hot water.

If your staff are comfortable and happy your business will run more smoothly and successfully.

The cubicles used for Treatment should be restful and airy, with a table and chairs placed near a window so that there is a good working light for the Manicurist.

The tables should be slightly higher than an ordinary table, to avoid straining the back. Twenty-eight to thirty inches is a good working height and a glass top measuring 20 inches by 33 inches is the most practical.

Across the centre of the table place a small, clean towel, or cushion and a glass tray containing all the necessary instruments. Bottles and jars should be on the right side of the Manicurist.

The daylight should be on the left-hand side of the Manicurist and electric light immediately over the table.

The Reception Salon should have a telephone and desk for making appointments, chairs for waiting clients, and magazines. The whole Salon should look attractive and inviting and should be spotlessly clean.

The Salon being ready to receive clients, assistants are necessary. An advertisement in the Trade Journals will usually bring a number of replies.

In choosing an assistant, remember it is better to have one really qualified assistant than six who know nothing about their work, and a professional test of their work should be made before employing them.

The terms of employment should be clearly understood by both parties.

A form can be obtained from Her Majesty's Stationery

Office which sets out the basic salary as laid down by the National Wages Council. It is usual to give commission on work and sales in addition to the basic wage.

After choosing an assistant, some time must be allowed for the assistant to learn the method employed by the Salon, so that all the assistants give a uniform treatment. This is especially useful when an assistant is away.

After a few months training in the method used by the Salon, it is a great advantage to the employer and also to the employee if an Agreement is entered into for a period of two or three years. This safeguards both parties and recompenses for the financial loss of the training period.

Clients are best obtained by advertisements in the personal columns of the daily papers and women's magazines, and business should gradually build up by recommendation.

Strict accounts must be kept and books maintained giving all the details of work and sales done. A good firm of Accountants must be employed in order to ascertain the financial progress of the business and advise on any matters concerning Government Departments.

A Licence from the London County Council is necessary when opening a Salon of this kind in London. This is renewed annually. Elsewhere Local Authorities grant Licences.

The Licence must be framed and hung up permanently, also a list of prices charged for various treatments should be easily seen by visitors to the Salon.

To protect the business against any unforeseen accident or claim an Insurance Policy covering this should be taken out and renewed yearly.

The staff employed should be courteous, efficient, tactful and enthusiastic, with a gentle, but assured, approach. They should all be similarly dressed in smart silk or nylon overalls and be well groomed.

If all the foregoing advice is taken and the Proprietor is prepared for hard work and constant vigilance a successful business can be built in about three years.

The Hand & Nail Institute was established in 1932, but it was not until 1942 that a research was made into nail disorders. This was due to the World War which commenced in 1939.

Many women during the war years used their hands for work that completely ruined their hands and nails; work in hospitals, canteens, munition and other factories, the Women's War Services, Ambulance and First Aid – to mention a few of their many contributions to the war effort.

Many of these women had never soiled their hands before and, during the war years, came to the Institute, or wrote in great distress.

Up to that time, the Institute had specialised in troublesome nails, but the need became so great for some real help where hands and nails were in a diseased condition that a special study was made in order to solve this problem and help the unfortunate women who were suffering much discomfort.

The results were encouraging and many women had their hands and nails completely restored.

The nail disorders dealt with in the following pages in no way represent a complete picture of the many fungi or conditions which bring about a destruction of the nailplate.

They are simply the disorders which are most commonplace and which the Manicurist should be able to recognise and, with her skill, relieve, improve and, in many cases, cure.

Doctors generally are so overworked and have little time to give to nail troubles that it comes as a relief to the sufferer who, by this time, has tried everything and failed to alleviate the disorder, to find that there really is a treatment available which will, in most cases, arrest and improve the condition; and in many cases, result in a complete recovery.

All the Treatments are based on experience gained over a long period of time with nails which were diseased – and gradually a daily routine and formulas were evolved which proved to be successful in arresting disorders and building up new, healthy nails and cuticle.

When failure to achieve this result was experienced, it was found that the daily routine had not been carried out conscientiously.

The general health, circulation, age, diet and vitamin intake were all found to be important. Extra multiple vitamins and minerals should be taken, especially Vitamin B 2 and D; and the diet should contain plenty of salads, fresh fruit, dairy produce and proteins.

Much of the treatment carried out at home is tedious and boring but it must be strictly adhered to if good results are desired; and proper nail hygiene practised for all time – to avoid recurrence of the disorder.

BREAKING NAILS.

Diagnosis. This is a trouble we hear so much about; nails which flake and break off at the slightest provocation and which will not stand up to ordinary wear and tear.

The nails lose their elasticity and flake away at the free-edge; they become brittle and dry and catch in everything.

A healthy, well nourished nail contains many substances in its make-up such as Arsenic, Keratin and Sulphur whereas breaking and flaking nails have a deficiency in these important elements.

Causes. There are many causes of breaking nails. Here are some important ones:

Hard chalky water.

Nail enamels which stain and dry up the nailplate.

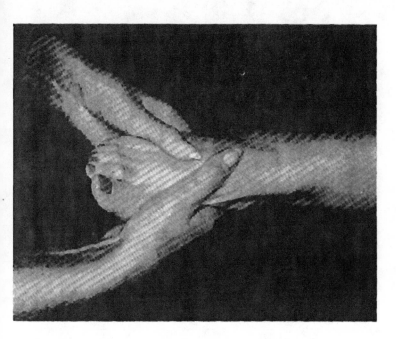

13 Massaging the foot (movement 7)

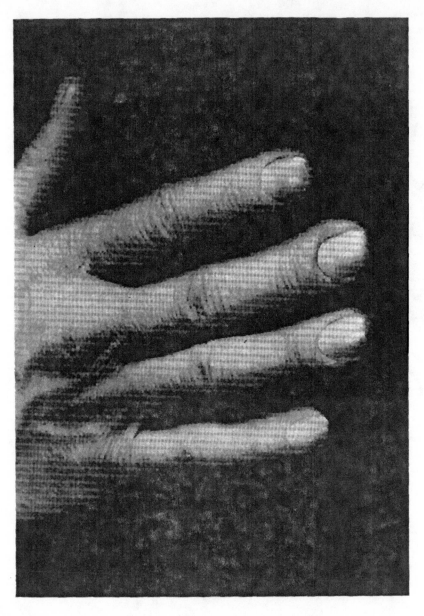

14 Paronychia—inflammation of the cuticle

Rheumatism and acidity.

Damage done to the embryo nail by injudicious digging into the cuticle, which causes the nails to become ridged.

Bath salts and frequent immersion in water.

Disinfectants in swimming pools.

Lack of Calcium.

Allowing the nails to become too long (this causes strain).

Cutting or filing away the sides of the nails.

Contact with disinfectants, strong lotions, soaps and soda.

General debility.

Shock and after-effects of illness.

Occupational wear and tear.

Nail infections.

A diet deficient in Vitamins, fresh vegetables, fruits, dairy produce and proteins.

Corrective treatment. The following equipment and preparations are necessary for the corrective treatment: cotton gloves, rubber gloves, Iodine X or A.O.2, Nail-o-wax, Nail tip food, Nail Restorer, Vitanail Food, Healthinale, Klenza.

1. Start by clipping the nails short and square. Remove the top surface of the nailplate all over gently with the flat side of an emery board and also remove any signs of flaking at the free-edge in the same way, with an emery board.

The nailplate will now look dull but it will absorb the nail foods more readily. Keep the nails short and square and dull for some weeks and gently remove the surface of the nailplate once a month.

2. Using a clear enamel such as Nail-o-wax, paint a fine line on the extreme tip of the free-edge of the nailplate and keep the tip of the free-edge of the nailplate permanently protected in this way. This will protect the tip of the free-edge from wear and tear, leaving the body of the nail free and clear to breathe and absorb the nail foods, which should be used alternately, as it was found that the nails respond more quickly when different types of nourishment were used alternately.

G

Where there is an allergy to nail enamel omit this part of the treatment.

3. Every night, on retiring, paint the nails with Iodine X. This is an iodine specially prepared to penetrate the nailplate and it does not stain so readily as ordinary iodine.

Do not use white iodine; it contains ammonia and will increase the breaking.

Allow Iodine X to dry and liberally apply one of the nail foods all over the nails and wear cotton gloves. Continue this treatment for several months.

Where there is an allergy to Iodine X: use A.O.2.

After three weeks omit Iodine X for several weeks and re-commence as before, but never omit the nail foods.

4. During the day the free-edge of the nailplate should be kept filled underneath with a nail food, such as tip-food, and every time the hands are removed from water apply a good emolient hand cream (not the vanishing type).

This is essential as water dries up the nailplate and hands.

The daily routine outlined elsewhere in this book should be followed and the Chapter on nails read carefully.

TROUBLESOME CUTICLES.

Diagnosis. Nearly all cuticle troubles are self inflicted or caused by bad manicure. The delicate tissue surrounding the nailplate becomes thick, unsightly, red, inflamed and often painful. Some cuticles stick to the nailplate and are pulled down as the nail grows.

The cuticle becomes dry and readily splits when it reaches the final point of stretching. These splits are not only painful but are a source of many nail infections.

Causes. Acidity and Rheumatism.

Unscientific cutting, which encourages the growth.

Liquid acid cuticle removers, which have a drying effect and are injurious to both nail and cuticle.

Allowing the cuticles to stick to the nails.

Pushing back the cuticle with a towel or any instrument; this causes inflammation and damages the embryo nail.

Hot water, soaps, soda.

Bad circulation.

Bad manicuring generally.

Occupational wear and tear.

Cuticle infections.

The habit some people have of unconsciously pushing back the cuticle with their fingers; this may go on for hours whilst at a theatre or cinema or whilst reading or feeling worried.

Corrective treatment. The following equipment and preparations are necessary for the corrective treatment: orange sticks, rubber gloves, cotton gloves, rubber-ended hoof stick, Nail-o-wax, Mannah 1, Klenza, Healthinale.

    1. Never push the cuticle back with a towel or any instrument. Use a rubber-ended hoof stick and apply cuticle emollient with it twice a day.

    At night be liberal with the emollient and wear loose cotton gloves.

    2. For thick, growing cuticles, professional treatment is necessary every seven days, and the method outlined in this book for *permanently diminishing the cuticles* must be used by the Manicurist.

    3. For split and cracked cuticles clip the loose skin away, disinfect and dry thoroughly; then apply liquid collodion or Nail-o-wax to the split parts and be prepared for it to sting any open cuts in the cuticle. Let it dry and apply a good cuticle emollient.

    4. Every time the hands have been in water apply a cuticle emollient to counteract the damaging effect of the water.

    5. Keep loose gloves on at the cinema or theatre, or when watching television or reading a book, so that it is impossible unconsciously to irritate the cuticle by pushing it back with the fingers.

6. The maintenance of healthy cuticles depends upon keeping the cuticle away from the nailplate. This must be done daily with a hoof stick and anti-acid cuticle emolient (not with cuticle remover); just as it is necessary to clean the teeth every day with a tooth paste so the cuticle needs daily clearance of the acid which it collects underneath.

The daily routine for hands and nails outlined elsewhere in this book should be followed, and the Chapter on *cuticles* read carefully.

LONGITUDINAL AND TRANSVERSE RIDGES.

Diagnosis. There are two kinds of ridges which appear on the nailplate, longitudinal and transverse.

Longitudinal ridges run from the half moon to the free-edge of the nailplate and gradually the nailplate becomes dry, brittle and distorted and the ridges are inclined, in time, to open up. Sometimes the longitudinal ridges appear as fine striated lines all over the nailplate with gradual deterioration and great discomfort. Longitudinal ridges can be greatly improved and the whole nail strengthened but when these ridges are striated and constitutional they cannot be entirely eradicated.

Transverse ridges run across the nailplate from one nail groove to the other and the nail sometimes appears broken in half. With transverse ridges the nailplate rapidly loses its shape and elasticity. Deep grooves appear and the whole surface of the nail is uneven. Transverse ridges can usually be completely cleared from the nailplate.

The whole nail must be well nourished day and night and sufficient time allowed for the ridges to grow out. This takes from one to six months and, with corrective treatment, the nails will eventually return to their normal condition.

Causes. Longitudinal ridges can be caused by rheumatism and acidity. Faulty circulation is a contributing factor and exterior damage can result in this type of ridge. When the ridges run in fine striated lines down the nailplate, they are caused by age and are constitutional, being equivalent to grey hair.

Transverse ridges can be the result of an illness, especially a high temperature which will ridge the embryo nail and the ridge will show as the nail grows. Another cause of transverse ridges is digging into the cuticle, which damages the embryo nail. Chilblains, when they swell up, press into the embryo nail and the nailplate will grow out with transverse ridges.

An accident or exterior damage of any kind can also result in this type of ridge.

Corrective treatment. The following equipment and preparations are necessary for the corrective treatment: emery boards, rubber-ended hoof-stick, adhesive tape, cotton gloves, rubber gloves, Iodine X, Nail tip food, Vitanail food, Klenza, Healthinale.

1. With the flat side of an emery board gently file the ridges away all over the nailplate. Do this once a month. The nailplate will look dull but it can be polished with a buffer.

If the longitudinal ridges are not filed down and the nailplate well nourished, they will eventually open up over a period of time and expose the live flesh.

The nailplate will be more comfortable when it has been made smooth and the ridges removed mechanically. Keep the nails short and square for some months.

2. If the ridges have opened up cover the open ridge with a very narrow strip of adhesive tape, just wide enough actually to cover the opening.

Seal this down with two coats of collodion or Nail-o-wax: Leave the remainder of the nailplate free to absorb nourishment.

As the nailplate becomes more nourished the open ridge will begin to heal up.

As the healing proceeds, make the adhesive strip smaller and narrower, so that ultimately there is a healed ridge with no adhesive tape on it.

3. Every night apply nourishing nail foods alternately and liberally all over the nails and wear loose cotton gloves.

4. During the day, wash the hands as little as possible and always apply an emolient cream afterwards.

For longitudinal ridges a nourishing diet and extra vitamins will help the nailplate.

5. For transverse ridges the cuticles must be left entirely alone for several months until the nailplate is smooth and clear, and the directions for *Troublesome Cuticles* carefully followed.

6. In cases where there is an open tranverse ridge due to an accident, and the nail appears to be in two pieces, do not remove the piece nearest to the free-edge. Often this is done and the upper half of the nail, as it grows down, has difficulty in growing over the tip of the finger where the piece of nail has been removed.

The nailplate keeps the flesh underneath it in shape; therefore, when a piece of the nailplate is removed the flesh becomes free and bulges, with the result that the growing nail cannot re-take its original perfect shape. Keep intact any portion of broken or ridged nail until it reaches the free-edge – then cut it away.

PARONYCHIA.

Diagnosis. This nail disorder is easily discernible: the cuticles are inflamed, red and swollen, often oozing pus, accompanied by throbbing and pain in the finger-tips. The condition can extend to the whole of the tissues surrounding the nailplate and, if neglected, can spread and inflame the finger, hand and arm. See Plate 14.

Causes. Paronychia is nearly always the result of exterior damage due to occupation such as housework, gardening or nursing, also immersion in soap, soda, water, wet substances, flour or any conditions which irritate the cuticle. It can also be caused by parasites, infection and bad manicure, and aggravated by cuticle removers.

It usually responds to suitable treatment and this should

be tried first, but in acute cases surgical intervention is sometimes necessary. Paronychia should not be neglected or it will eventually attack the nail matrix and this results in permanent injury to the nailplate.

Corrective treatment. The following equipment and preparations are necessary for the corrective treatment: cotton fingerstalls, roll of half-inch adhesive gauze, cellotape, cotton gloves, rubber gloves, rubber-ended hoof-stick, Neutralizer, A.P.1, A.P.2, A.P.3, Klenza, Healthinale.

As this disorder is recurrent, and can easily flare up again, avoid anything which can cause inflammation. The delicate tissues surrounding the nail should be suitably soothed and nourished – to protect them and it is important to keep the nail and cuticle in their natural groove. Never push the cuticle back; never file or cut the corners of the nail away; never dig when cleaning the nail.

Proper nail care *after* the condition is better is essential and suitable emolients should be used every day to prevent recurrence.

Night. Apply liberally the Anti-Paronychia ointments on alternate nights to the infected cuticles. Make small pads of cotton wool to cover the cuticles and nails. Dip the pads in cold water and press them flat and make them a convenient size (pad should cover cuticle) and liberally soak the pads with Anti-Paronychia lotion 3, and bind each pad over the inflamed cuticles with a strip of self-adhesive gauze half an inch wide, not too tightly, but firm enough to keep the pads on. Secure the end of the bandage with a small piece of cellotape.

If the binding is too tight it will cause throbbing. The gauze should not adhere to the region of the inflamed cuticle; the pads and ointment will prevent this. Buy the gauze wide enough to well overlap and secure the pads, and keep the pads on by binding them to the nails (not the cuticles) allowing the pads to overlap on to the cuticles from the nail.

When all the affected cuticles are bandaged, apply

Healthinale to the other nails and a good hand cream to the hands; and put on a pair of large, loose cotton gloves.

Keep a small basin of cold water by the side of the bed and if the cuticles throb during the night dip the fingers in this to re-wet the pads. Sleep with the arms bent upwards from the elbows.

This will relieve the throbbing, pain and inflammation.

After re-wetting the pads dry the surrounding skin and cream it; continue this treatment every night until all the throbbing and inflammation has subsided.

When the cuticles are better Healthinale should be applied all over the cuticles and nails every night, and loose gloves worn.

Day. Leave the cuticles bound up. They can be re-bound once every 24 hours at night only, or night and morning, if desired. The hands can be gently washed and dried with the pads on, and Healthinale applied to all exposed nails and surrounding tissues.

Re-wet the pads frequently during the day by dipping the finger-tips in cold water. The wet pads and preparations will draw out the pus and inflammation and relieve the throbbing and pain.

Continue this treatment as long as the inflammation lasts.

After a few weeks as the cuticles improve bind the pads on at night only.

Keep the hands and nails out of soap and water. If this is not possible use rubber gloves for periods of not more than 15 minutes at a time, and line the rubber gloves with a pair of thin cotton gloves to avoid contact with the rubber.

Use Klenza as much as you can to wash your hands instead of soap and water.

The cuticles must be left entirely alone and no instrument used anywhere near them; they should be allowed to grow until all the inflammation has subsided.

As the cuticles subside smear them several times a day, very gently, with Healthinale and later, when they are normal, apply Healthinale very gently underneath them every day with a rubber-ended hoof-stick to prevent further trouble. When the cuticles have grown and are flat the dead rim should be gently lifted away from the nail and only *one half* of this dead rim trimmed away: the other remaining half must be left to protect the live flesh.

If this small dead rim is not left the Paronychia *will flare up again* immediately.

This special method of diminishing the cuticle is fully explained in the chapter on *Cuticles*.

It sometimes happens in cases of Paronychia that all the cuticles clear up with the exception of one or two. When this occurs it may be caused by the bandage being too tight, or too large, thereby covering too much nail and cuticle and impeding the circulation and excluding air.

When this condition persists make the adhesive gauze looser and narrower and wear a loose cotton finger-stall.

When the inflammation has spread further than the cuticle, sometimes to the entire finger, enlarge the pad and use the preparations liberally so that they cover all the inflammation, and keep the pad wet by dipping it into cold water.

When the inflammation is restricted to the cuticle apply cold water to the pad in that area only, so that the palm side of the finger-tip is dry.

Where inflammation exists, the preparations and wet compress will open the pores and relieve the condition, but where inflammation does not exist, the wet compress will shrivel up the skin and take away the natural oils.

So where you notice the healthy flesh affected by the wet compress, apply Healthinale and restrict the compress to the area of the inflammation.

It cannot be emphasized too much that any rough treatment, accidental knock or immersion in soap and water will bring on the trouble again, and in the case of Cooks, House-workers or similar occupations, it is sometimes necessary to change one's occupation as Paronychia can result in the total loss of nail or even finger.

The cuticle in some cases may be slow to respond, and patience with the pads and preparations is necessary.

Some cases of Paronychia will clear in three weeks; other cases may take as long as six months.

When the intermediate stage has been reached, that is, when the acute inflammation has gone, and the pads are being used at night only, it is a good plan during the day to keep plenty of Healthinale smeared all over the cuticles and nails and wear loose gloves for work and play.

WARNING: Never use adhesive plaster, adhesive tape or rubber finger-stalls for any nail or cuticle trouble, as they seal the trouble in. Use only adhesive gauze, which is porous.

SUMMARY: *Night and morning.*

1. Keep some Neutralizer in a spray and use as a hand lotion every time after washing the hands; allow the Neutralizer to dry in.

When the infection has cleared continue using Neutralizer to prevent recurrence. Neutralizer is essential for skin hygiene; it counteracts the effects of soap and water, which feed the infection.

The infection is more active in hot weather, so use plenty of Neutralizer.

When the Paronychia is very sensitive dilute the Neutralizer with sufficient water to prevent a stinging sensation. It should not be diluted with more than 50 per cent water. Decrease water as the Paronychia improves until the Neutralizer is being used at full strength.

2. Pour some Neutralizer into a small jar and soak the nails about three minutes; allow it to dry in. Keep the Neutralizer in a suitable jar with lid well screwed on and it can be used again.

3. Apply Klenza all over the hands and wipe off.

4. As previously directed apply Ointments 1 and 2 alternately to infected cuticles. Saturate pads of cotton wool in Lotion 3 and bind each cuticle up with the pads and

self-adhesive gauze. Secure the gauze with a small piece of cellotape.

5. Apply Healthinale to all non-infected cuticles and nails.

6. When the infection has subsided it is essential to continue with Neutralizer, Klenza and Healthinale to prevent recurrence.

Extra treatment (night). When the infection is stubborn and slow to improve, in addition to the foregoing treatment the following *extra* treatment will help the cuticle to return to normal.

Every night, after carrying out the Summary instructions, wring out a Turkish towel large enough to cover the hands in cold water. A guest towel is a good size. Enclose all the bandaged finger tips in this, wrapping the wet towel completely round them, and then cover the wet towel with a dry one and keep the towels on with a bandage. The fingers and thumb should be touching each other, but not tightly.

This extra compress will, in many cases, be found most soothing and healing.

ONYCHIA.

Diagnosis. Onychia is a disturbance of the nailplate. Accompanying the condition there often appears to be dirt round the nailplate and in it, in various shades of discoloration such as grey, green, brown, black, white or a mixture of these. See Plate 16a.

The discoloration is not dirt, but fungus. Gradually the fungus spreads and separates the nailplate from its bed; the nailplate becomes distorted in shape and deteriorates in texture and strength.

When Onychia is not checked Ringworm often develops: a much more serious disturbance which eventually destroys the nailplate and matrix.

Causes. Onychia is often the result of direct fungus infection of the nailplate but can be caused by exterior damage. It frequently follows Paronychia: the cuticle infection gradually spreading and invading the nailplate. It can also be caused by skin diseases such as Psoriasis or Eczema.

Psoriasis is a type of nail infection which causes great nail deterioration. It is easily recognised in its early stages by tiny pittings or holes resembling a thimble, and fine transverse lines on the nailplate. In its later stages the nail separates from the finger and usually becomes discoloured.

Eczema is a type of nail disturbance with most destructive features. It can usually be recognised by the odorous and weeping condition underneath the nailplate, with rapid deterioration of the whole nail. It will be found that the sufferer is not in a good state of health and is in need of constitutional treatment from a doctor.

Corrective treatment. The following equipment and preparations are necessary for the corrective treatment: emery boards, rubber gloves, rubber-ended hoof-stick, Iodine X or A.O.5, Neutralizer, A.O.2, A.O.3, Klenza, Healthinale.

The nails should be kept short and square, and as much nail as possible cut and filed away at first, in order to remove mechanically the affected part.

The top surface of the nailplate should be gently removed with an emery board so that the nailplate looks dull. It will absorb the remedies more readily.

As it takes six months to grow a new nail, this time should be allowed for results, although great improvement is often experienced in a matter of weeks. It depends largely on the cause of the Onychia.

Mechanical movements on the nails and cuticles, such as filing and trimming, should be very gentle. They should not hurt in any way or the nail trouble is likely to get worse.

Where either Paronychia or Onychia have existed for some time the nail matrix may be affected, causing subsequent discoloration and malformation of the nailplate, so it is important to give the nails early and regular treatment to avoid this.

When the condition is neglected or wrongly treated permanent injury can result to the nails. Suitable treatment will be found of inestimable value even when the injury is of a permanent nature.

In the following treatment Iodine X is advised. This should not, however, be used if the sufferer is allergic to Iodine. In such cases Iodine X should be replaced by Anti-Onychia 5, otherwise Iodine X is extremely beneficial and should be used immediately the cuticles are normal.

In some cases of simple fungus when the nail is separated from the finger and gloves are worn at night with ointment, the separation increases.

When this occurs the ointment should be applied *without* wearing gloves.

Attention is specially drawn to the danger of increasing the infection in hot weather by using cream and gloves at night, or getting face creams, cooking fat, flour etc., into the free-edge of the nailplate.

Care should be taken when the weather is hot to avoid oils and creams.

Healthinale, which is anti-fungus, smeared on the nails and cuticles, without gloves, and Klenza used on the hands, will *not* increase the infection or separation of the nailplate, and it is a most important part of the treatment that they be used daily.

For the effect of oils and creams on some forms of fungus infection, such as Ringworm, read the chapter on Ringworm.

SUMMARY : *Night and morning.*

1. Keep some Neutralizer in a spray and use after washing the hands. Allow the Neutralizer to dry in. When the infection has cleared continue using Neutralizer to prevent recurrence.

Neutralizer is essential for skin hygiene. The fungus is more active in hot weather and water feeds it, so use plenty of Neutralizer.

2. Pour some Neutralizer into a small jar and soak the infected nails about 3 minutes; allow to dry in.

The Neutralizer should be kept in a suitable jar with lid well screwed on and can be used again.

3. Apply Klenza all over the hands and wipe off. Keep Klenza away from the nails.

4. Paint nails on top and under the free-edge (with cotton wool on the tip of an orange stick) with: A.O.2 in the morning; A.O.3 at mid-day; Iodine X at night.

Where there is an allergy to iodine smear a little Healthinale on the cuticle and surrounding tissue before apply Iodine X – or use A.O.5.

5. Apply a small amount of Healthinale on cuticles and nails after using the tinctures and wipe surplus away.

If the cuticle is very sensitive apply a smear of Healthinale and wipe off before using the tinctures as well as after using them.

6. Use rubber gloves for all wet work; cotton gloves for all dry work. Avoid water, grease, oils, face creams, lotions of all kinds getting in contact with the nails as these feed Onychia and will increase its activity.

While the fungus is active wear outdoor gloves as little as possible and do not wear sleeping gloves at night.

Gloves and nail enamels enclose, increase and feed the fungus.

Use Healthinale and Klenza very sparingly until the infection has cleared. Avoid all other emollients.

7. When the infection has cleared, to keep the nails healthy, it is essential to continue with Neutralizer, Healthinale and Klenza.

These constitute the minimum for Hand and Nail Hygiene.

Remember, the fungus infection will re-appear given the soil it likes to live on.

WARNING: Never use adhesive plaster, adhesive tape or nail enamel when there is any nail or cuticle trouble as they seal the trouble in. To replace adhesive tape use adhesive gauze which is porous.

PARONYCHIA AND ONYCHIA COMBINED. In many instances these two conditions are present together. When this is the case the Paronychia must be treated first and then the

Onychia later, because the Onychia preparations are not suitable for an infected cuticle.

Where these two conditions are found at the same time it indicates that the infection has been active for a long period and may take many months to clear; at least six to twelve months should be allowed for the condition to subside, and this could extend to a much longer period.

ONYCHOPHAGIA (NAIL BITING).

Diagnosis. The nails have no free-edge and look embedded in the flesh of the finger-tip. The surrounding tissues of the nailplate often appear red and inflamed. The nailplate loses its function of controlling the shape of the finger-tip and in some cases of Onychophagia the nailplate becomes so embedded that the finger-tip looks bulbous.

Causes. This unsightly and irritating habit is often caused by dryness of the cuticle and weak nails which break off. Combined with nervous tension and worry, the cuticle and nail disturbance annoys the owner beyond endurance and causes them either to bite or push the nail and cuticle.

Contrary to the general belief that people who bite their nails are usually bad tempered, the reverse is the case. They are generally people of artistic and generous natures, scrupulously clean and tidy and cannot bear imperfection or disorder, and the habit springs from these very qualities.

Corrective treatment. The following equipment and preparations are necessary for the corrective treatment: cotton gloves, rubber-ended hoof-stick, Onux, Nail-o-wax, Oily enamel remover, Vitanail food, Nail Restorer, Klenza, Healthinale.

Bitter aloes and other nasty tasting lotions applied to the nails do not treat the *cause* and therefore are seldom successful. The nails should be made strong with a suitable food applied at night and gloves worn. This will also heal the cuticle.

Any loose pieces of nail or skin should be clipped away and a coat of clear enamel painted on the edge of the nailplate often proves helpful as its presence reminds the sufferer that they are biting a foreign substance as well as the nail.

Gloves should be worn as much as possible both for work and leisure especially at night when reading or visiting a theatre or cinema or watching television, as they act as a deterrent.

Sometimes the habit is overcome more easily if, leaving all the remaining nails alone, the sufferer is persuaded to concentrate on biting one nail only; preferably the nail of the little finger.

The nine remaining nails, when cured, act as a spur and encourage the sufferer to give up the habit entirely.

Regular manicures are a great help as they remove some of the causes of the irritation. If it is not possible to have professional help, regular care at home will greatly help the condition.

Where Onychophagia has existed for a long period, it will be found almost impossible to grow the nail over the swollen flesh of the finger. To make this easier and encourage the growth – fine wisps of cotton wool saturated with Healthinale should be forced between the nail edge and the flesh.

This will be difficult at first as there will be no free-edge to the nail, but as the nail grows it will be possible to insert this fine packing.

Keep it there night and day and pack it in gently with the fine end of an orange stick.

Do not injure the nail bed. This packing will allow the nail to grow over the bulbous part more easily and should be borne with until the nail has recovered its normal shape and size.

When the nails have recovered, a regular routine to nourish the hands and nails is essential.

SUMMARY: *Day and night.*

> *Note*: Onux is an anti-nail biting tincture made by the Hand and Nail Culture Institute. It should not be used on very young children – who might rub their eyes and inflame them. For young children follow the treatment as directed but omit using Onux.

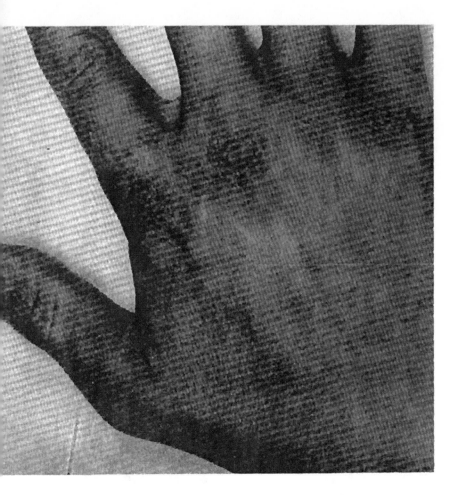

15 Ringworm

16a   Onychia—fungus infection of the nailplate

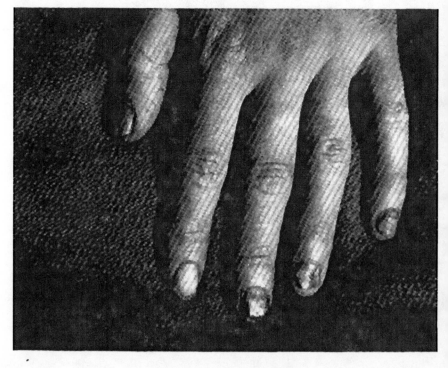

16b   Ringworm

Day: Trim any roughness of the nail away with an emery board. Paint Onux on, not more than one-third of the nail from the free-edge, leaving two-thirds of the nail free to absorb the nail foods.

Apply Healthinale to the cuticles with a hoof-stick. (Well shake the Onux bottle each time before using.) Use a camel hair brush to apply it. Clean the brush immediately afterwards in an enamel remover. Leave the nails about ten minutes to dry.

Night: Very gently try to apply Healthinale underneath the free-edge of the nail with an orange stick.

Apply Nail Restorer and Vitanail Food all over the nails on alternate nights and wear gloves.

Follow *General Rules for Hand and Nail Care.*

LEUKONYCHIA (White spots).

Diagnosis. There are many theories for these disfiguring spots which appear for no apparent reason in small, or large numbers all over the nailplate. They usually occur in nails which are weak or of delicate texture. The spots are sometimes opaque and sometimes white; the rest of the nail and cuticle appears healthy but fragile.

Causes. Many children are told that these white spots denote a similar number of presents they will receive, but it is only an 'old wives' tale'.

The spots are actually caused by external injury which, in turn, causes a separation in the nail cells and allows air to permeate the cells.

Harsh manicuring, external knocks, or pressure on the nailplate, typing, playing the piano and games generally can cause this separation when the nailplate is not strong enough to stand up to these activities.

Another possible cause is acid, which collects underneath the cuticle and grows out with the nail. The acid becomes attached to the nailplate and is visible as white spots.

Corrective treatment. The following equipment and preparations are necessary for the corrective treatment: cotton gloves, rubber gloves, rubber-ended hoof-stick, Iodine X,

H

Nail Tip Food, Vitanail food, Nail Restorer, Klenza, Healthinale.

When the cause is exterior damage, then, naturally, every care must be taken to avoid injury to the nailplate. Where the nails are of delicate texture they must be protected and nourished regularly.

When the white spots are due to acidity the cuticle must be gently lifted and cleared and the acid gently scraped away so that it cannot grow out with the nailplate.

General daily care of the hands and nails is helpful to this condition.

Iodine X applied to the nailplate will stimulate the healthy cells to work and toughen the nailplate at the same time.

It should be used in conjunction with the nail foods to counteract its drying effect.

SUMMARY:

Night: Wrap cotton wool round the tip of an orange stick and paint the nails with Iodine X. Allow a few minutes for it to dry and then apply Nail Restorer and Vitanail Food alternately, and wear loose cotton gloves.

Day: Use Healthinale and Klenza as directed and keep the free-edge of the nail filled permanently with Nail Tip Food. Use cotton gloves for all dry work and rubber gloves for wet work.

SOFT, THIN, BENDING NAILS.

Diagnosis. The nails appear healthy but are often devoid of a free-edge, because the nailplate will not stand up to ordinary wear and tear. The nails refuse to grow to any reasonable length; the nailplate looks fragile and is some-times soft to the touch; the nails and finger-tips are sensitive and uncomfortable.

Causes. This type of nail trouble is most difficult to treat because the condition is constitutional. The skin generally is abnormally thin and fine and often depleted of its full number of layers.

Corrective treatment. The following equipment and pre-parations are necessary for the corrective treatment: cotton gloves, rubber gloves, Nail Hardener, M 304 Lotion, Nail-o-wax, Nail Restorer, Nail Tip Food, Klenza, Healthinale.

It is essential in these cases that, in addition to external treatment, the whole system should be built up.

Multiple vitamins and minerals are indicated; Wheat germ, Calcium, Halibut oil and a balanced diet of Protein, Salads, Fruit and Dairy produce are necessary to build up the general health.

This condition is slow in responding to treatment. Nail enamel and Cuticle removers will increase the trouble and should be avoided. False nails seal the natural nails up and prevent them from breathing or receiving any exterior nourishment.

Unfortunately, as the condition is constitutional, the trouble can never be entirely eradicated, but it can be greatly helped, and nail foods which have hardening properties and those which contain certain substances which are deficient in the nailplate, such as Keratin and Sulphur, should be constantly applied.

SUMMARY: *Night.*

1. Empty lotion M 304 into a screw top jar.

2. Dip all nails into this for three minutes. Remove, and allow the lotion to dry on the nails.

3. Apply Nail Hardener and Nail Restorer on alternate nights liberally all over the nails and wear loose cotton gloves.

Morning.

1. After washing apply Klenza to the hands and Healthinale to the cuticles.

2. Dip nails in M 304 and allow to dry. Apply Nail Tip Food.

3. Keep the tip of the free-edge of the nails covered with a coat of Nail-o-wax (to protect them) leaving the body of the nailplate clear to absorb the remedies. Allow ten minutes for the Nail-o-wax to thoroughly dry.

4. Rubber gloves should be worn for all wet work, and loose cotton gloves for all dry work.

TINEA (Ringworm).

Diagnosis. This infection is the most tenacious of all nail disorders. It usually starts at the free-edge of the nailplate and, by a process of sometimes swift deterioration, eats away the nail edge; gradually the nail becomes discoloured, thick, the nailplate becomes separated from the nail bed, with red inflamed cuticles (without pus). See Plate 15.

In some cases the nail appears to be growing normally at the cuticle, but about one third of the way along disintegrates. It sometimes comes off completely.

In due course the free-edge at the finger-tip becomes more and more eaten away and, eventually, there is a thick diseased nail, half, or one third, of the original size, with only unformed, hard, striated pieces of the remaining part.

This worm-eaten process continues from nail to nail and often spreads to the hands, causing them to become red and infected. See Plate 16b.

It is much more violent in its action than any other fungi peculiar to nails – the main difference being the space between the nailplate and the finger-tip which looks worm eaten, and the eventual invasion of both cuticles and hands.

Causes. Ringworm is usually caused by exterior damage to the nails, the damaged tissue then coming into contact with the infection through animals, gardening or nursing and is quite often found in persons with a tubercular history.

Corrective treatment. The following equipment and preparations are necessary for the corrective treatment: small finger bowl, rubber fingerstalls, box of wooden sticks, cotton gloves, rubber gloves, castor oil, Neutralizer, bottle of disinfectant (R.D.5), R.N. 6, Klenza or R.E. 7, Healthinale.

Over a period of years a non-paying Clinic was established at the Hand and Nail Culture Institute in order to study this most virulent type of nail infection and it was found impossible to make progress unless constant attention was given to the smallest detail.

It was established that the main causes of the persistence of this fungus was *re-infection* and exterior damage, and it took a great deal of trial and error to evolve a routine for the sufferer which was practical and efficient, as no amount of mechanical treatment, or application of remedies, were effective without a *non-re-infection* routine.

This, indeed, is the operative essential in treating Ringworm. Failure on the part of the patient to carry out the routine for even a day results in wasted time and effort.

Next in importance comes exterior damage. Damaged tissue encourages the fungus to eat into the nails at an alarming rate.

Foremost must be placed grease or oil of any kind whether in cosmetic or in ointment form, or even in neutralised fats of any description.

Ringworm lives and thrives in grease, water and damaged tissue. Destruction of the nailplate is certain and sometimes swift if all grease is not eliminated from exterior contact with the nailplate, or what is left of it. Water was also found to feed the fungus.

Great strides were made when these two substances, grease and water, were prevented from coming into contact with the Ringworm.

Lastly, exterior damage proper, such as removal of the whole nailplate, or damage incidental to the patient's work, or life; or, again, probing the cuticle. Ringworm was found to be more active after any of these conditions.

It follows, therefore, that any mechanical removal of parts of the infected nailplate must be very gentle. The whole nail should never be removed, but it is helpful gently to clip and file the diseased part away as much as possible, so that the treatment is speeded up.

The treatment takes six to twelve months, or longer, although great improvement will be experienced in two or three months; it depends on the age of the patient and history of the case. Two cases under the following treatment cleared up in four months.

All the remedies used are limited to a spirit base; no water base or ointment of any kind are permitted. The treatment or routine must not be altered in any way as this would render it ineffective.

Any soreness or dryness must be borne patiently.

It is only in the event of an adverse reaction to the acid employed that any oil be used – and then castor oil exclusively.

One problem is dryness of the hands and nails due to the large quantity of drying and disinfecting liquids used in the routine, but the skin will harden up to these in due course with no ill effects.

The dryness must be endured as part of the treatment.

When the infection has cleared the patient should always use a neutralizing medium after washing, to prevent recurrence, and suitably prepared hand and nail preparations.

All Ringworm patients have been found to be sceptical and depressed because they have tried so many means of recovery, without result. Even when the nails have started to show marked improvement in colour and texture the patient seems to take a pessimistic view to the bitter end.

Sufferers seem almost afraid to admit they can see any improvement. One patient, who was cured in four months, began, towards the end of the treatment, to neglect the long soaking in the Neutralizer which is an essential part of the Routine, until he noticed the deterioration which resulted, even in a single day. Immediately he soaked the nails in the Neutralizer again they became a healthier colour.

The routine for Ringworm will arrest, improve and is essential for this fungus, but will not effect a cure.

Theoglycollic Acid, which makes the nail unpalatable for the Tinea (ringworm) to eat must be applied every seventh day, and more often on hard nailplates.

This acid looks harmless but if used inexpertly can destroy the nailplate entirely. Only one drop is needed for each application which should be given by a Doctor or an expert conversant with its action.

Full details for its application and an Antidote are given later in this Chapter.

As a matter of interest a routine devised by a patient and approved by the writer is also included, as well as the routine recommended by the Institute.

There are, of course, antibiotics which deal with this distressing infection internally but the writer feels that every external medium should be tried first before resorting to antibiotics, as often antibiotic treatment can have an undesirable effect on the general health of the sufferer.

In some cases antibiotics are completely successful with no visible ill effects and a simple routine of Neutralizer, Klenza, and R.E. 7 will be found all that is necessary to keep the infection in check.

SUMMARY: *Night and morning.*

1. No soap, water, grease to touch the nails. These feed the fungus. Use rubber gloves for all wet work and bathing. To avoid re-infection use cotton gloves for dry work and for lining outdoor gloves.

2. If imperative, wash your hands not more than once a day. Add 1 teaspoon of R.D.5 to water and wash and dry the hands quickly. Then saturate them with Neutralizer, using a spray. Allow Neutralizer to dry in.

At other times wash the hands with Neutralizer only. When the infection has improved or cleared, never omit using Neutralizer – to prevent recurrence. Neutralizer is essential for skin hygiene.

3. Pour some Neutralizer into a small jar and soak all the nails from three to ten minutes and allow to dry. Throw the used Neutralizer away each time.

4. Using cotton wool on the tip of a wooden stick apply R.N.6 to infected nails only. Do not touch the flesh. Strong nails: once a day; weak nails every other day. Do not re-dip the stick in R.N.6, and throw away the stick after use. Apply Healthinale to non-infected nails.

5. After a few weeks – if the condition is sufficiently arrested and the hands are uncomfortably dry – apply a little Klenza with a soft paper tissue and wipe the

surplus away. Do not touch the nails with Klenza.

When the hands, as well as nails, are infected do not use Klenza until the infection has cleared. Instead, rub in a very little R.E.7 on hands only. Later, when the Ringworm is weakened R.E.7 may be used to build up the nailplate.

The Ringworm should be watched carefully for any sign of renewed activity and R.E.7 omitted until such time as the nailplate can absorb it without increased invasion by the Ringworm.

6. Disinfect everything you have been using with R.D.5 – 1 teaspoon to a bowl of water – to prevent re-infection, i.e., jar, rubber gloves, outdoor gloves, towels, etc.

7. Theoglycollic Acid should be applied, as directed, once every seven days on women's nails and two or three times a week on men's nails (see Special Directions).

The acid is not active after seven days.

Directions for Applying Theoglycollic Acid.

1. Cut or clip all you can of the infected nail away, then file the top surface of the nail away with an emery board and throw the emery board away.

2. Have ready a large piece of paper, a small wooden stick and the acid.

3. Dip the wooden stick into the bottle so that you have not more than one drop on the stick, and apply to the middle portion of the infected part of the nail and only where the nailplate is hard. One dip should be enough for all the infected nails.

To avoid re-infection do not re-dip the stick into the acid.

Use a fresh stick every time.

Do not touch the flesh, cuticle or surrounding tissue. Do not spill the acid.

Do this over the large sheet of paper. When finished, wrap up the stick in the paper and throw away.

Great care is needed as the acid can be harmful if not used correctly, and has a strong, unpleasant odour.
4. If there is any reaction which you consider excessive, such as acute inflammation of the surrounding tissues, soak the nail in Neutralizer. If you feel you need something more use the Theoglycollic Acid *antidote*.

Many patients have no reaction. Some feel a slight pulling or tightening. This is normal and not harmful.
5. One drop of acid on the nailplate spreads all over it, as if putting a drop of ink on blotting paper.
6. It is possible for the smell of the acid to cause *nausea*. Avoid this by sitting near an open window. Do not enclose the nails in gloves or bedclothes afterwards. The acid should be kept in a bathroom or outhouse away from the reach of children.

WARNING : *Theoglycollic Acid is highly dangerous if not used with great care and will burn everything it touches.*

The finger-nails will have an unpleasant odour after using the acid but this is unavoidable.

An application is necessary every seven days as the acid loses its effect after that period.

NOTE : Theoglycollic Acid should not be sent through the Post or handled by inexperienced Operators.

Theoglycollic Acid Antidote

If by accident the acid is spilt or runs on to the skin, apply Theoglycollic Acid Antidote as follows:
1. To 1 part of Hydrogen Peroxide (strength 10 volumes) add 3 parts of water (i.e. 1 teaspoon of Hydrogen to 3 teaspoons of water). Mix in a small vessel.

Dip nails in for a few seconds, allow to dry. When necessary, apply to the skin with a pad of cotton wool.
2. Saturate pads of cotton wool with A.P.3 or calomine lotion and bandage loosely on to the nails or affected part. Frequently re-wet the compress with A.P.3 without

undoing the compress. Keep on day and night. Re-new compress every 24 hours or as desired.

3. When the condition subsides, smear on a minimum of castor oil.

From a ringworm patient

The following routine was devised by a patient who had Ringworm in one finger and was cured after attending the Hand and Nail Institute four months.

The Ringworm started after she had scrubbed the floor of a large room and caused exterior damage to her hands and nails.

Received from a Patient, August 28th, 1955:

'I have a small tray in my bedroom on which I put everything I am likely to need:

Bottle of R.D.5 : Bottle of R.N.6 : Box of wooden sticks : Large bottle of Neutralizer : Small finger bowl
Rubber fingerstall.

I also keep a bottle of Neutralizer in the office, on top of my desk so that I shan't forget to use it when I wash my hands.

I found that the quickest and easiest way for me to carry out the routine was as follows:

I got up earlier by ten minutes in the morning. After soaking my nails in Neutralizer and using R.N.6 on cotton wool on the end of a wooden stick, which I threw away together with the used Neutralizer, I filled the bowl with water to which I added disinfectant R.D.5 and left the bowl and disinfected water on the tray for the rest of the day.

At home at night I put on a fingerstall to bath in, stripped it off when finished. I then soaked my finger for ten minutes in Neutralizer, using the same routine as morning. I again filled the bowl with water and disinfectant R.D.5, put the fingerstall in it and left it overnight.